BIRMINGHAM IN 50 BUILDINGS

LORNA TALBOTT

AMBERLEY

First published 2021

Amberley Publishing, The Hill, Stroud
Gloucestershire GL5 4EP

www.amberley-books.com

British Library Cataloguing in Publication Data.
A catalogue record for this book is available from the British Library.

ISBN 978 1 3981 0311 5 (print)
ISBN 978 1 3981 0312 2 (ebook)

Typesetting by SJmagic DESIGN SERVICES, India.
Printed in Great Britain.

Contents

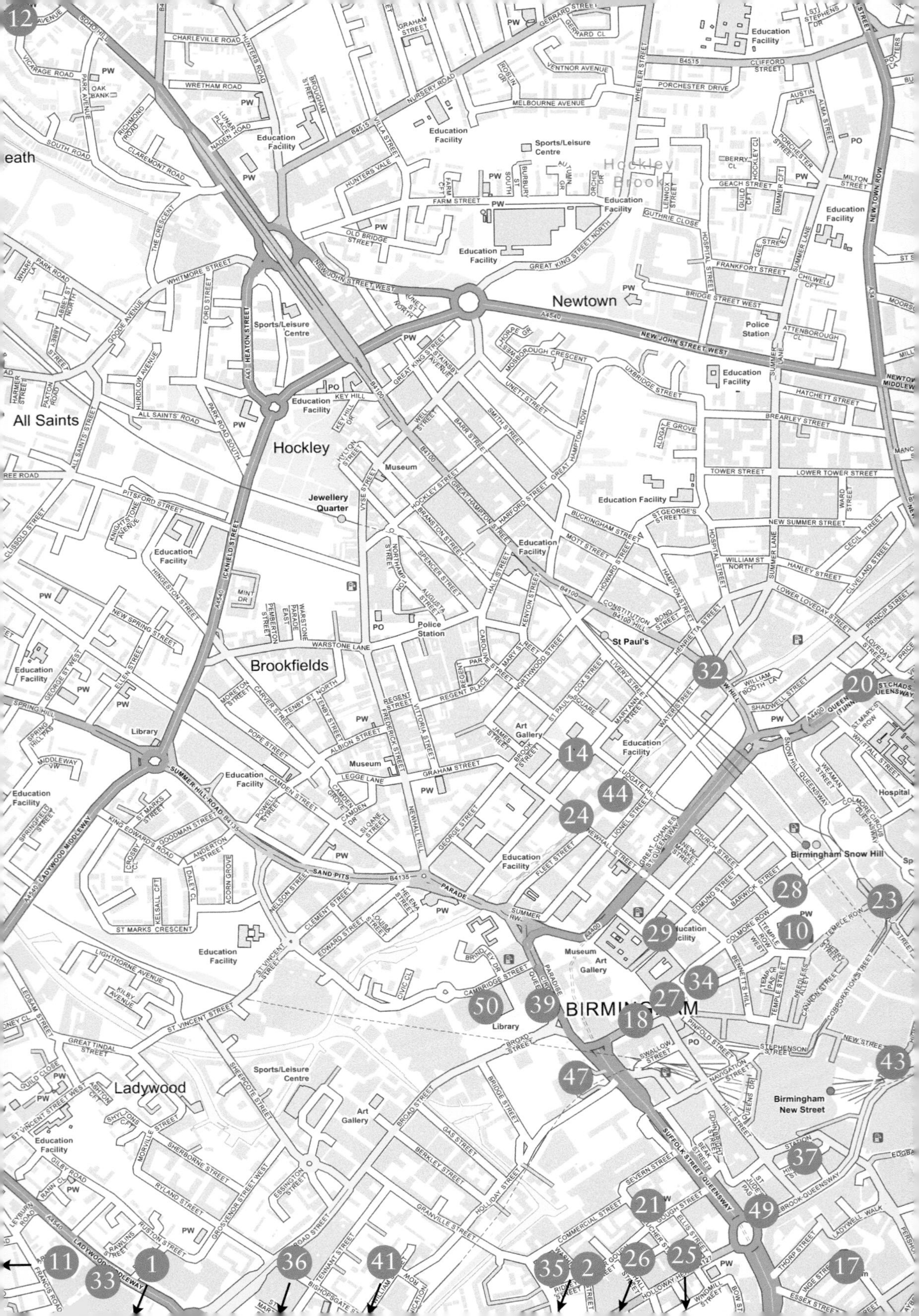

12
CHARLEVILLE ROAD
HUNTERS ROAD
VICARAGE ROAD
PARK AVENUE
OAK BANK
WRETHAM ROAD
RICHMOND ROAD
SOUTH ROAD
CLAREMONT ROAD
LUNAR PLACE
NADEN ROAD
Education Facility
BROUGHAM STREET
GRAHAM STREET
NURSERY ROAD
VILLA STREET
B4515
Education Facility
GERRARD STREET
GERRARD CL
VENTNOR AVENUE
ROSLIN GR
MELBOURNE AVENUE
WHEELER STREET
PORCHESTER DRIVE
CLIFFORD STREET
Education Facility
ST STEPHENS DR
Sports/Leisure Centre
Hockley Brook
AUSTIN LA
ALMA STREET
BERRY CL
HOCKLEY CL
PORCHESTER STREET
MILTON STREET
NEW TOWN ROW
A34
HUNTERS VALE
FARM CFT
FARM STREET
SOUTH ST
BURBURY ST
AUTUMN GR
ORCHID DR
LENNOX STREET
GUTHRIE CLOSE
GEACH STREET
GUILD CFT
SUMMER CFT
Education Facility
OLD BRIDGE STREET
Education Facility
GREAT KING STREET NORTH
HOSPITAL STREET
GEE STREET
SUMMER LANE
FRANKFORT STREET
CHILWELL CFT
eath
PARK ROAD
THE CRESCENT
WHARF LA
WHITMORE STREET
ABBEY ST NORTH
ABBEY STREET
GOODE AVENUE
FORD STREET
HEATON STREET
A41
Sports/Leisure Centre
NEW JOHN STREET WEST
TUNELL ST NORTH
Newtown
BRIDGE STREET WEST
Police Station
A4540
NEW JOHN STREET WEST
ATTENBOROUGH CL
HARMER STREET
PAXTON ROAD
HURDLOW AVENUE
PARK ROAD SOUTH
KEY HILL
KEY HILL DR
Education Facility
GREAT KING STREET
STAINSBY AVENUE
HORACE GR
MOSBOROUGH CRESCENT
UNETT STREET
UXBRIDGE STREET
Education Facility
NEWTOWN MIDDLEWAY
HATCHETT STREET
BREARLEY STREET
All Saints
ALL SAINTS STREET
ALL SAINTS' ROAD
Hockley
WELL STREET
BARR STREET
SMITH STREET
GREAT HAMPTON ROW
ALDGATE GROVE
TOWER STREET
LOWER TOWER STREET
WARD STREET
REE ROAD
PITSFORD STREET
HYLTON STREET
Museum
Jewellery Quarter
HOCKLEY STREET
GREAT HAMPTON STREET
HARFORD STREET
BUCKINGHAM STREET
ST GEORGE'S STREET
Education Facility
NEW SUMMER STREET
CLISSOLD STREET
KNIGHTSTONE AVENUE
Education Facility
ICKNIELD STREET
A4540
VYSE STREET
BRANSTON STREET
NORTHAMPTON STREET
SPENCER STREET
Education Facility
MOTT STREET
HOWARD STREET
HAMPTON STREET
WILLIAM ST NORTH
HANLEY STREET
CECIL STREET
CLEVELAND STREET
HINGESTON STREET
MINT DR
PEMBERTON STREET
EAST PARADE
WARSTONE PARADE
AUGUSTA STREET
PO
Police Station
HALL STREET
KENYON STREET
B4100
CONSTITUTION HILL
BOND STREET
HENRIETTA STREET
LOWER LOVEDAY STREET
PRINCIP STREET
NEW SPRING STREET
WARSTONE LANE
St Paul's
LOVEDAY STREET
Education Facility
GEORGE ST WEST
ELLEN STREET
Brookfields
CAROLINE STREET
MARY STREET
NORTHWOOD STREET
LIVERY STREET
32
WILLIAM BOOTH LA
20
ST CHADS QUEENSWAY
SPRING HILL
SPRING HILL PAS
Library
MORETON STREET
CARVER STREET
TENBY ST NORTH
TENBY STREET
REGENT STREET
VITTORIA STREET
REGENT PLACE
ST PAUL'S SQUARE
COX STREET
MARY ANN STREET
WATER STREET
SHADWELL STREET
A4400
QUEENSWAY TUNNEL
ST MARY'S ROW
WHITTALL STREET
MIDDLEWAY VW
POPE STREET
ALBION STREET
FREDERICK STREET
Art Gallery
JAMES STREET
BROOK STREET
14
Education Facility
SNOW HILL QUEENSWAY
WEAMAN STREET
Education Facility
SPRINGFIELD STREET
ST MARKS STREET
SUMMER HILL ROAD
B4135
Education Facility
CAMDEN STREET
Museum
LEGGE LANE
GRAHAM STREET
44
LUDGATE HILL
Hospital
COLMORE CIRCUS QUEENSWAY
KING EDWARD'S ROAD
GOODMAN STREET
CAMDEN GROVE
CAMDEN DR
POWELL STREET
SLOANE STREET
NEWHALL HILL
GEORGE STREET
24
LIONEL STREET
GREAT CHARLES ST QUEENSWAY
CHURCH STREET
NEWMARKET STREET
Birmingham Snow Hill
LADYWOOD MIDDLEWAY
A4540
CROSBY CL
ANDERTON STREET
DALEY CL
ACORN GROVE
SAND PITS
B4135
PARADE
Education Facility
FLEET STREET
NEWHALL STREET
EDMUND STREET
BARWICK STREET
28
23
KELSALL CFT
NELSON STREET
CLEMENT STREET
HELENA STREET
LOUISA STREET
SUMMER ROW
A4400
29
Education Facility
COLMORE ROW
TEMPLE ROW WEST
10
TEMPLE ROW
ST MARKS CRESCENT
EDWARD STREET
Education Facility
ST VINCENT STREET
BRINDLEY DR
Museum
Art Gallery
PARADISE CIRC
QUEENSWAY
BENNETT'S HILL
CHERRY STREET
LIGHTHORNE AVENUE
KILBY AVENUE
CIVIC CL
CAMBRIDGE STREET
34
TEMPLE PAS
TEMPLE STREET
NEEDLESS ALLEY
CANNON STREET
CORPORATION STREET
50
Library
39
27
BIRMINGHAM
18
PINFOLD STREET
PO
NEW STREET
43
LEDSAM STREET
ST VINCENT STREET
BROAD STREET
SWALLOW STREET
STEPHENSON STREET
GREAT TINDAL STREET
Sports/Leisure Centre
47
NAVIGATION STREET
QUEENS DR
GUILD CLOSE
ASHTON CFT
Ladywood
SHEEPCOTE STREET
BRIDGE STREET
Birmingham New Street
ST VINCENT STREET WEST
SHYLTONS CFT
Art Gallery
BROAD STREET
GAS STREET
HILL STREET
JOHN BRIGHT STREET
BEAK STREET
Education Facility
MORVILLE STREET
SHERBORNE STREET
BERKLEY STREET
SUFFOLK STREET QUEENSWAY
STATION STREET
37
EDGBASTON
GILBY ROAD
RANN CL
ESSINGTON STREET
SEVERN STREET
ST JUDE'S PAS
HILL ST
SMALLBROOK QUEENSWAY
RYLAND STREET
GROSVENOR STREET WEST
HOLLIDAY STREET
21
GOUGH STREET
49
COMMERCIAL STREET
GRANVILLE STREET
ELLIS STREET
LADYWELL WALK
LEYBURN ROAD
A4540
RAWLINS STREET
RUSTON STREET
THORP STREET
11
LADYWOOD MIDDLEWAY
1
33
FRANCIS ROAD
36
BISHOPSGATE ST
TENNANT STREET
41
35
2
26
25
HOLLOWAY HEAD
WINDMILL STREET
BOW ST
17
INGE STREET
ESSEX STREET

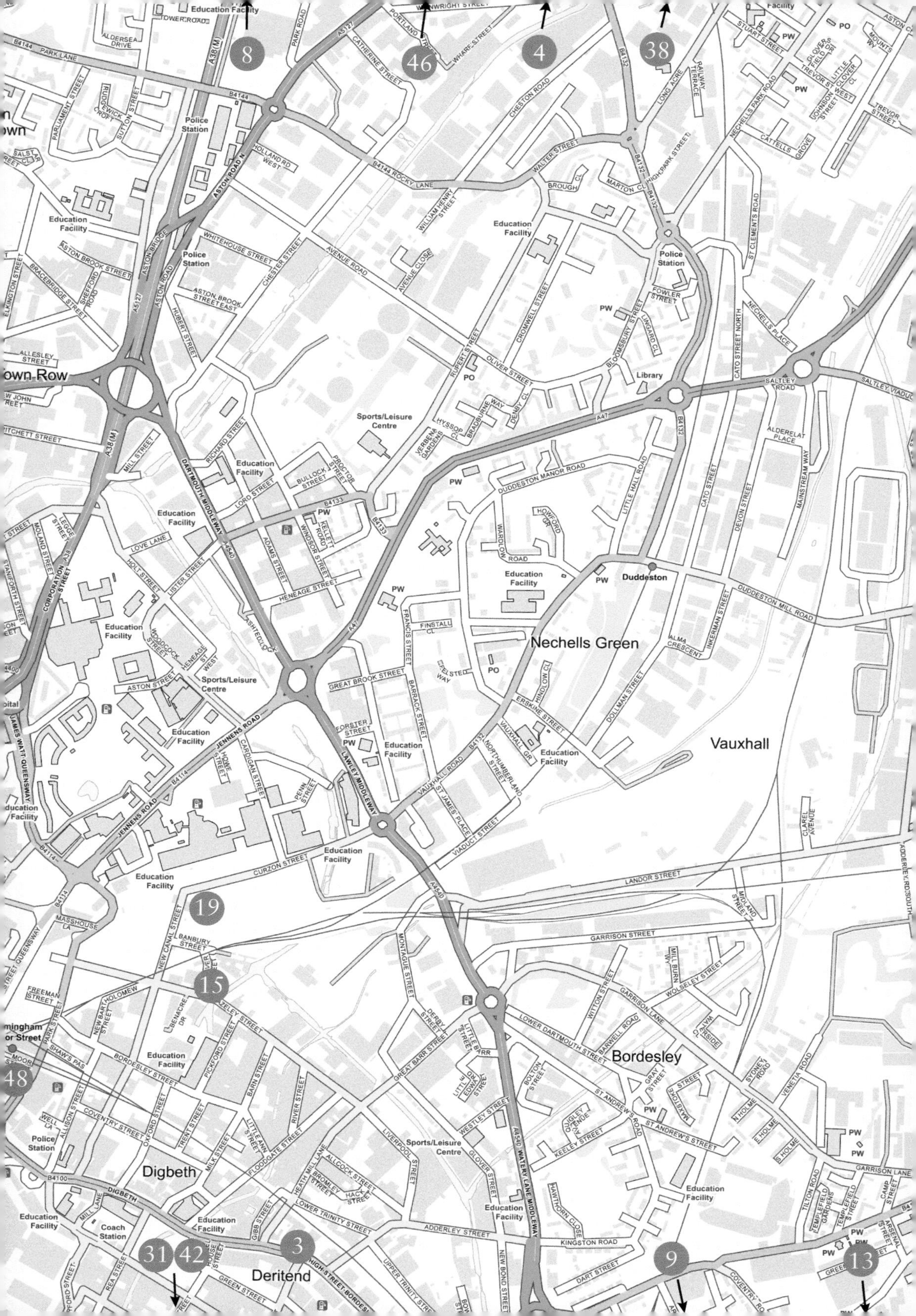

Education Facility
TOWER ROAD
ALDERSEA DRIVE
PARK LANE
A38(M)
PARK ROAD
A5127
CATHERINE STREET
PORTLAND STREET
WHARF STREET
WAINWRIGHT STREET
8
46
4
38
B4132
LONG ACRE
RAILWAY TERRACE
Facility
PO
PW
STUART STREET
GLOVERS FIELD DR
TREVOR ST
LITTLE CLOVER
MOUNTS WAY
ASTON CH
NECHELLS PARK ROAD
JOHNSON STREET
WEST
CL
TREVOR STREET
CATTELLS GROVE
PARLIAMENT STREET
RUDGEWICK CROFT
SUTTON STREET
B4144
Police Station
CHESTON ROAD
SALSTAR CL
HOLLAND RD WEST
ASTON ROAD N
B4144 ROCKY LANE
WALTER STREET
HIGH PARK STREET
BROUGH CL
MARTON CL
WILLIAM HENRY STREET
Education Facility
ST CLEMENTS ROAD
WHITEHOUSE STREET
ASTON BRIDGE
AVENUE ROAD
AVENUE CLOSE
ASTON BROOK STREET
BRACEBRIDGE STREET
SHEFFORD ROAD
ELKINGTON STREET
ASTON ROAD
A5127
CHESTER ROAD
ASTON BROOK STREET EAST
HUBERT STREET
CROMWELL STREET
FOWLER STREET
LINGARD CL
BLOOMSBURY STREET
NECHELLS PLACE
CATO STREET NORTH
ALLESLEY STREET
Town Row
NEW JOHN STREET
RUPERT STREET
OLIVER STREET
Library
SALTLEY ROAD
SALTLEY VIADUCT
MITCHETT STREET
A38(M)
MILL STREET
Sports/Leisure Centre
HYSSOP CL
VERBENA GARDENS
BRADBURNE WAY
DENBY CL
A47
B4132
ALDERFLAT PLACE
RICHARD STREET
DARTMOUTH MIDDLEWAY
PROCTOR STREET
BULLOCK STREET
LORD STREET
DUDDESTON MANOR ROAD
LITTLE HALL ROAD
CATO STREET
DEVON STREET
MAINSTREAM WAY
LEGGE STREET
MOLAND STREET
LOVE LANE
B4133
KELLETT ROAD
WINDSOR STREET
ADAMS STREET
HOWFORD GR
WARDLOW ROAD
A4540
CORPORATION STREET
A38
HOLT STREET
LISTER STREET
HENEAGE STREET
Duddeston
DUDDESTON MILL ROAD
STANIFORTH STREET
FINSTALL CL
FRANCIS STREET
Nechells Green
INKERMAN STREET
ALMA CRESCENT
WOODCOCK STREET
ASHTED LOCK
HENEAGE ST WEST
ASTON STREET
GREAT BROOK STREET
BARRACK STREET
KELSTEDWAY
HINDLOW CL
DOLLMAN STREET
ERSKINE STREET
JAMES WATT QUEENSWAY
JENNENS ROAD
HOWE STREET
CARDIGAN STREET
FORSTER STREET
LAWLEY MIDDLEWAY
VAUXHALL ROAD
VAUXHALL GR
NORTHUMBERLAND STREET
Vauxhall
B4114
PENN STREET
ST JAMES PLACE
VIADUCT STREET
CLAREL AVENUE
CURZON STREET
LANDOR STREET
ADDERLEY RD SOUTH
19
MIDLAND STREET
MASSHOUSE LA
NEW CANAL STREET
BANBURY STREET
GARRISON STREET
MONTAGUE STREET
MILL BURN WAY
FREEMAN STREET
NEW BARTHOLOMEW STREET
15
WITTON STREET
GARRISON LANE
WOLSELEY STREET
BENACRE DR
PICKFORD STREET
LITTLE BARR
BARWELL ROAD
LOWER DARTMOUTH STREET
ERSIDE
Bordesley
SHAW'S PAS
BORDESLEY STREET
GREAT BARR STREET
DERBY STREET
BOLTON STREET
GRAY STREET
SYDNEY ROAD
VENETIA ROAD
48
BARN STREET
RIVER STREET
ALLISON STREET
COVENTRY STREET
OXFORD STREET
TRENT STREET
LITTLE ANN STREET
EDWARD STREET
WESTLEY STREET
QUIGLEY AVENUE
ST ANDREW'S ROAD
ST ANDREW'S STREET
MAXSTOKE STREET
N HOLME
E HOLME
S HOLME
WELL LA
MILK STREET
FLOODGATE STREET
LIVERPOOL STREET
Sports/Leisure Centre
GLOVER STREET
KEELEY STREET
Digbeth
HEATH MILL LANE
ALLCOCK STREET
BROMLEY STREET
HACK STREET
HAWTHORN CLOSE
TILTON ROAD
TEMPLEFIELD GARDENS
TEMPLEFIELD STREET
CAMP STREET
B4100
DIGBETH
MILL LANE
Coach Station
GIBB STREET
LOWER TRINITY STREET
A4540 WATERY LANE MIDDLEWAY
ARSENAL STREET
Education Facility
ADDERLEY STREET
KINGSTON ROAD
31
42
3
9
13
REA STREET
HIGH STREET BORDESLEY
UPPER TRINITY STREET
NEW BOND STREET
DART STREET
COVENTRY RD
Deritend
GREEN STREET

Key

1. St Laurence's Church
2. Minworth Greaves and Selly Manor
3. The Old Crown
4. The Lad in the Lane
5. Old Grammar School
6. Tudor Merchants House
7. Blakesley Hall
8. Aston Hall
9. Church of the Ascension
10. St Philip's Cathedral
11. Perrott's Folly
12. Soho House
13. Sarehole Mill
14. St Paul's Church
15. Birmingham Gun Barrel Proof House
16. Kings Norton Stop Lock
17. Birmingham Back to Backs
18. Town Hall
19. Curzon Street Railway Station and Principal Building
20. St Chad's Cathedral
21. Singer's Hill Synagogue
22. St Martin in the Bullring
23. Great Western Arcade
24. Assay Office
25. Highbury Hall
26. Cadbury Chocolate Factory
27. Council House
28. Grand Hotel
29. Birmingham School of Art
30. Victoria Law Courts
31. Balsall Heath Library and Baths
32. The Red Palace, Nos 1–7 Constitution Hill
33. No. 21 Yately Road
34. Nos 122–124 Colmore Row
35. Bournville Junior School and Carillon
36. University of Birmingham
37. The Electric Theatre
38. Fort Dunlop
39. Hall of Memory
40. Odeon Cinema
41. Barber Institute of Fine Arts
42. Wake Green Prefabs
43. The Rotunda
44. BT Tower
45. Our Lady Help of Christians
46. Gravelly Hill Interchange – Spaghetti Junction
47. Alpha Tower
48. Selfridge's Building
49. Beetham Tower
50. Library of Birmingham

Introduction

Architecturally, most of Birmingham dates from three historical periods. There are factories from the Industrial Revolution, large Victorian buildings displaying civic pride and innovative designs marking the redevelopment of the city in the twentieth and twenty-first centuries.

However, the history of Birmingham began, like much of Great Britain, in the Stone Age. Although a few scattered tribes used the land for hunting and foraging, there was no proper settlement in the area until the Anglo-Saxons arrived. The Beormingas tribe settled on an area of fertile land in the seventh century and named it Beormingaham. In its listing in the *Domesday Book* of 1086, 'Bermingeham' is described as being a village of little value. However, a market charter granted to it in 1166 gradually brought prosperity due to merchants visiting the town. The strong network of tracks and roads developed by traders for easy transportation of goods ultimately led to Birmingham becoming the successful and cosmopolitan city it is today.

The Birmingham area was rich in iron ore, and when a coal seam was discovered it enabled the use of furnaces for smelting. By the seventeenth century a burgeoning metal industry had begun. As Birmingham already had good roads and a nationally central position, it was the ideal site for development. When the Industrial Revolution began, Birmingham led the country in progressive manufacturing and urbanisation.

There are a few fragments of medieval Birmingham left, although some of these, like Selly Hall, have been moved from their original site as the town expanded and the land was needed for development. Other properties still exist as they have for centuries and their Georgian and Victorian splendour has become enveloped

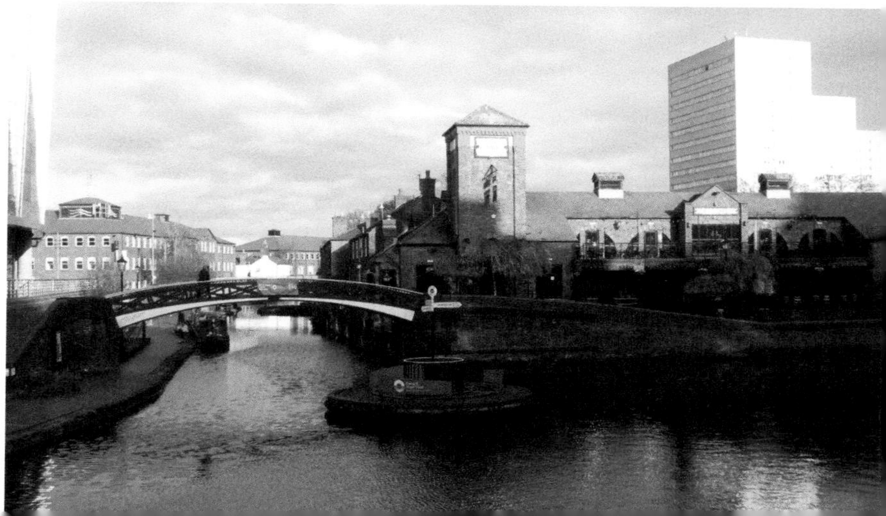

The waterways of Birmingham were created during the Industrial Revolution.

by the growing city. Birmingham is constantly changing and redevelopment is continual. It is therefore fortunate that many of its historically interesting buildings are protected for future generations by having listed status from Historic England.

As England's second city and a major centre of manufacture, Birmingham has given the world Cadbury's chocolate, Bird's custard and Typhoo tea. Birmingham was also the home of the Arts and Crafts movement, whose signature styling has impacted the architectural legacy of the city.

Birmingham in 50 Buildings looks at the earliest churches and dwellings in the city and unique pieces of industrial heritage. It explores municipal structures, art deco cinemas and iconic shopping centres. Birmingham is built on its commercial and industrial past and by studying just fifty of its fascinating buildings, the city's history is uncovered.

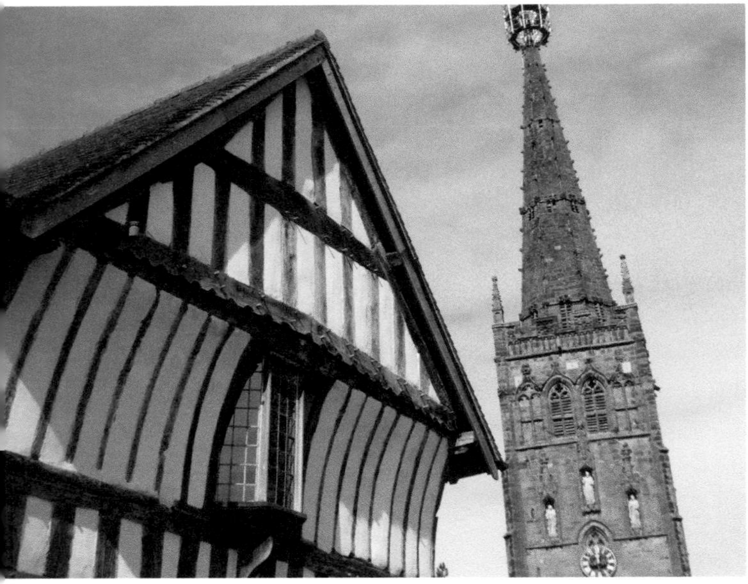

Birmingham still has many of its interesting medieval buildings.

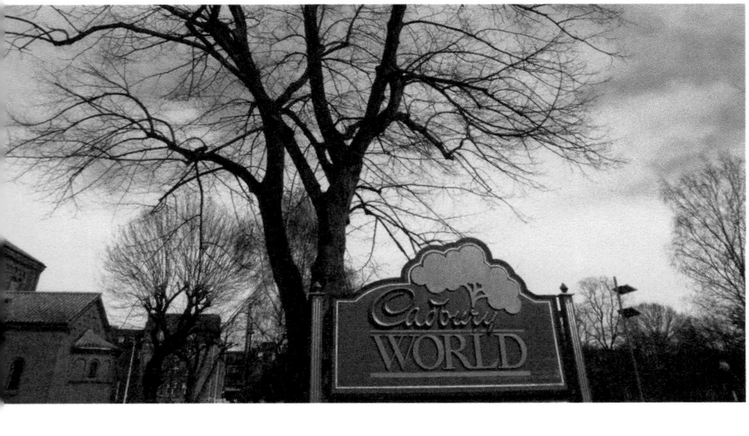

Birmingham has always been the producer of leading brands.

The 50 Buildings

1. St Laurence's Church (*c.* 1170)

The ancient St Laurence's Church in Northfield is the oldest building in the Birmingham area. It was built after the market charter given to Birmingham brought in enough prosperity for construction of a stone church.

The oldest part of the building is the doorway with its characteristic Norman zig-zag decorations. There are carved stone heads, also of early Norman origin, which were moved from the nave and set into the tower when the church was rebuilt in 1230. In the fifteenth century further alterations included the addition of the upper portion of the tower and the timber porch.

St Laurence's has decorative features from the Norman period.

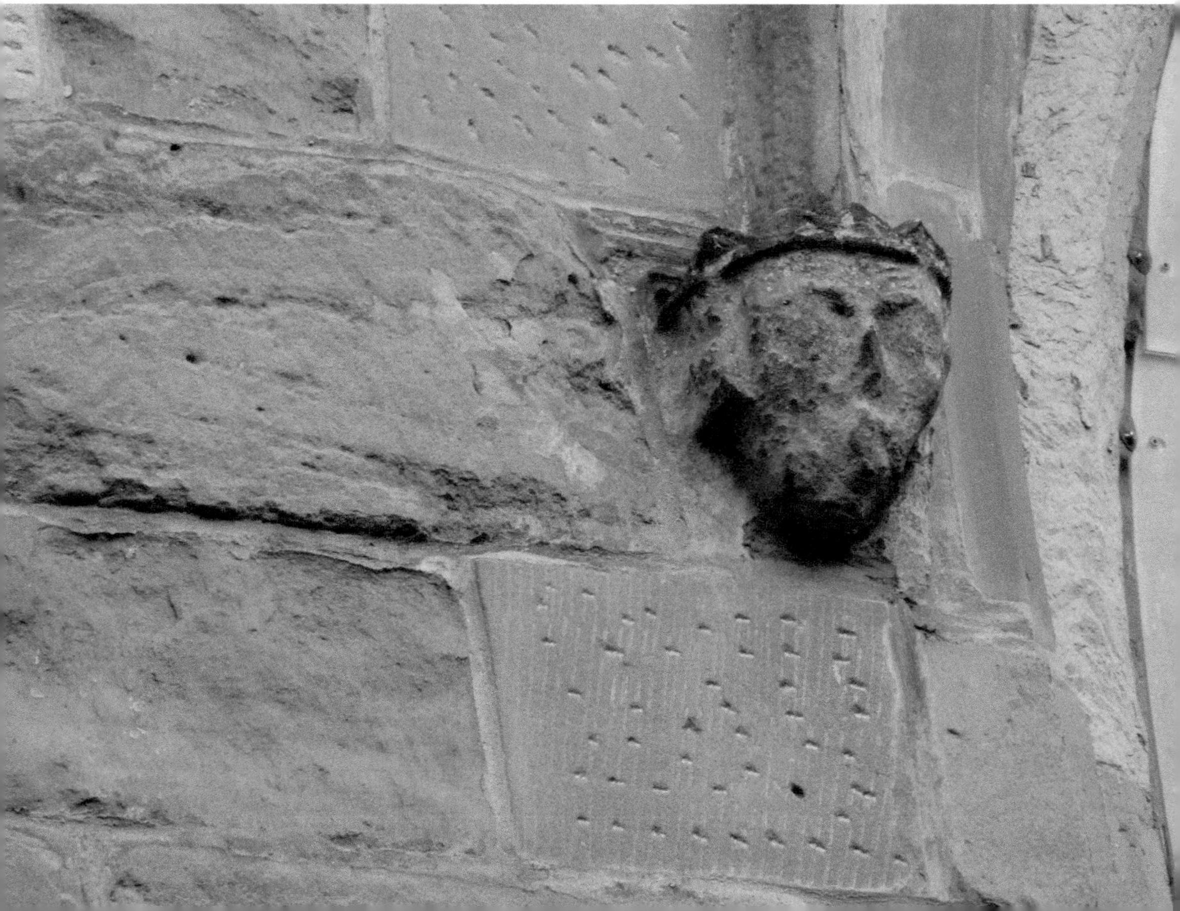

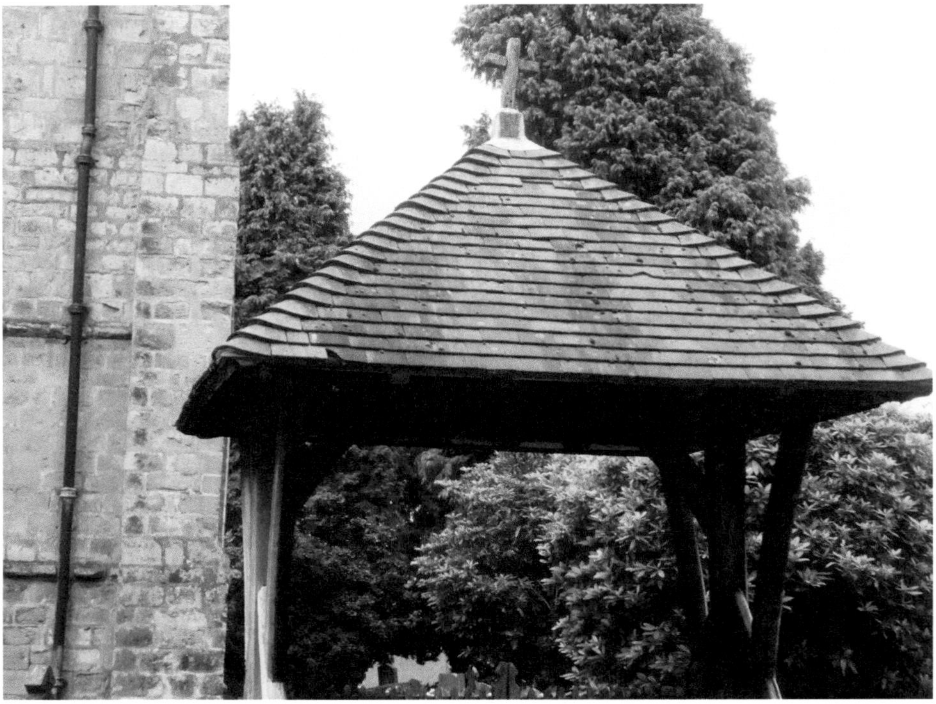

The lychgate is medieval in origin.

St Laurence's Church has been given a Grade I listing from Historic England due to its ancient architectural features. The interior structure has some unusual medieval characteristics, including a thirteenth-century priest's door with original tympanum in the chancel. Upon removal of damaged plaster, a faint trace of medieval painting was discovered on this arched frieze. Subsequent restoration revealed that it is a 'doom painting' of the last judgement. Similar depictions were often used in medieval churches to remind the congregation of their mortality.

The nave is lined with stone-framed lancet windows set with Victorian stained glass, one of which was designed by eminent cathedral architect Augustus Welby Northmore Pugin.

The wall around the churchyard has remained intact since its medieval construction and contains a well-preserved lychgate. It has a Grade II listing from Historic England.

2. Minworth Greaves and Selly Manor (*c.* 1250/1476)

Minworth Greaves and Selly Manor are the two ancient houses that together form Selly Manor Museum. The museum was set up by philanthropist George Cadbury after he rescued the two structures from demolition and moved them piece by piece to

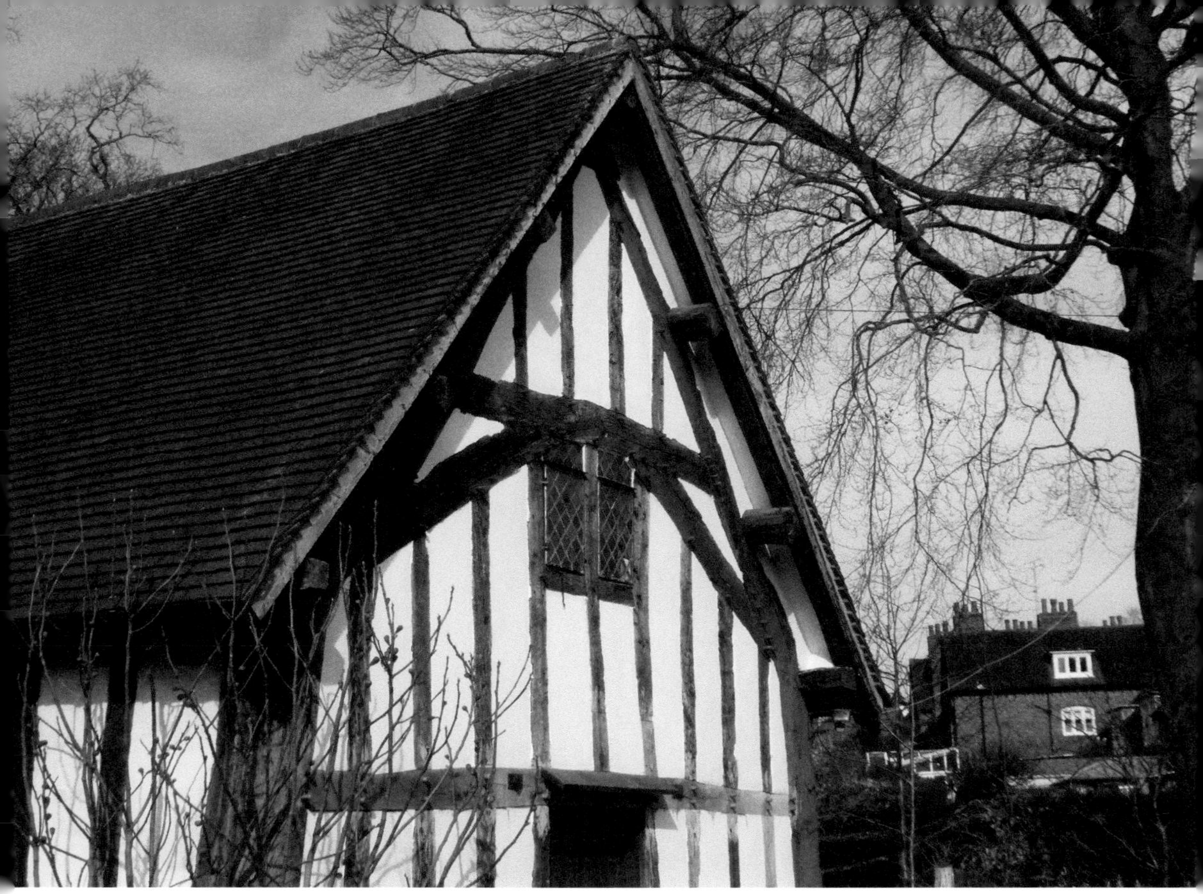

Minworth Greaves was originally built during the thirteenth century.

Bournville village. The museum, on the corner of Sycamore and Maple Roads, opened in 1916 and both buildings were later given a Grade II listing by Historic England.

Minworth Greaves is a simple cruck frame cottage originally built in the thirteenth century in a nearby village. Over the centuries the cottage changed and the timber frame was clad in brick. The building grew in size and the timbers remained unseen for centuries.

In the early twentieth century, the growing need for more housing sparked a growth in suburban sprawl. When the vastly altered crook cottage was swallowed by developments and due to be demolished, George Cadbury discovered it had an ancient core and purchased it to save the thirteenth-century timber skeleton.

The medieval home was recreated in Bournville by putting a timber frame with plaster infill around the original crook and using reclaimed medieval tiles for the roof. It now stands next to Selly Manor, which Cadbury moved from Selly Oak and rebuilt in a similar project.

Selly Manor was built in 1476 and had a succession of prosperous farming tenants. When the style of the house became unfashionable during the seventeenth century, landlords allowed it to fall into disrepair. Selly Manor was nearly derelict when it was purchased by George Cadbury for restoration.

Every timber, brick and tile in the house was carefully dismantled and rebuilt in Bournville. The meticulously restored Selly Manor now houses a museum of Tudor life.

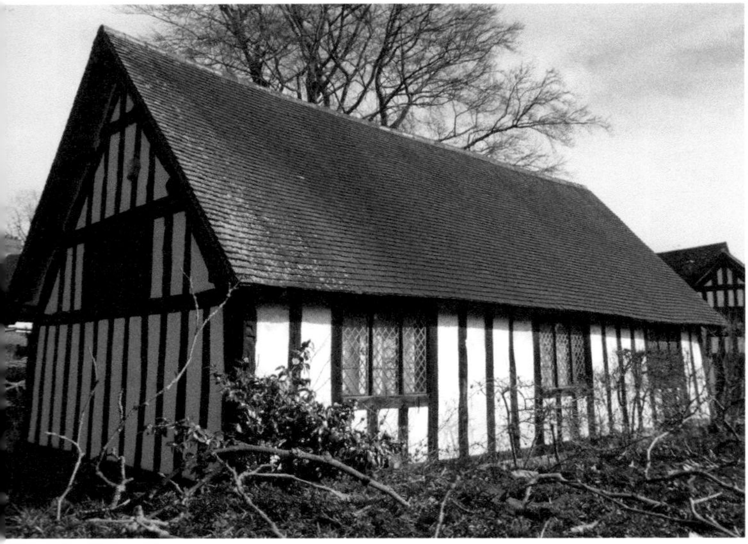

Left: The ancient cottage was restored over a century ago.

Below: Jettied Selly Manor was built for wealthy Tudor farmers.

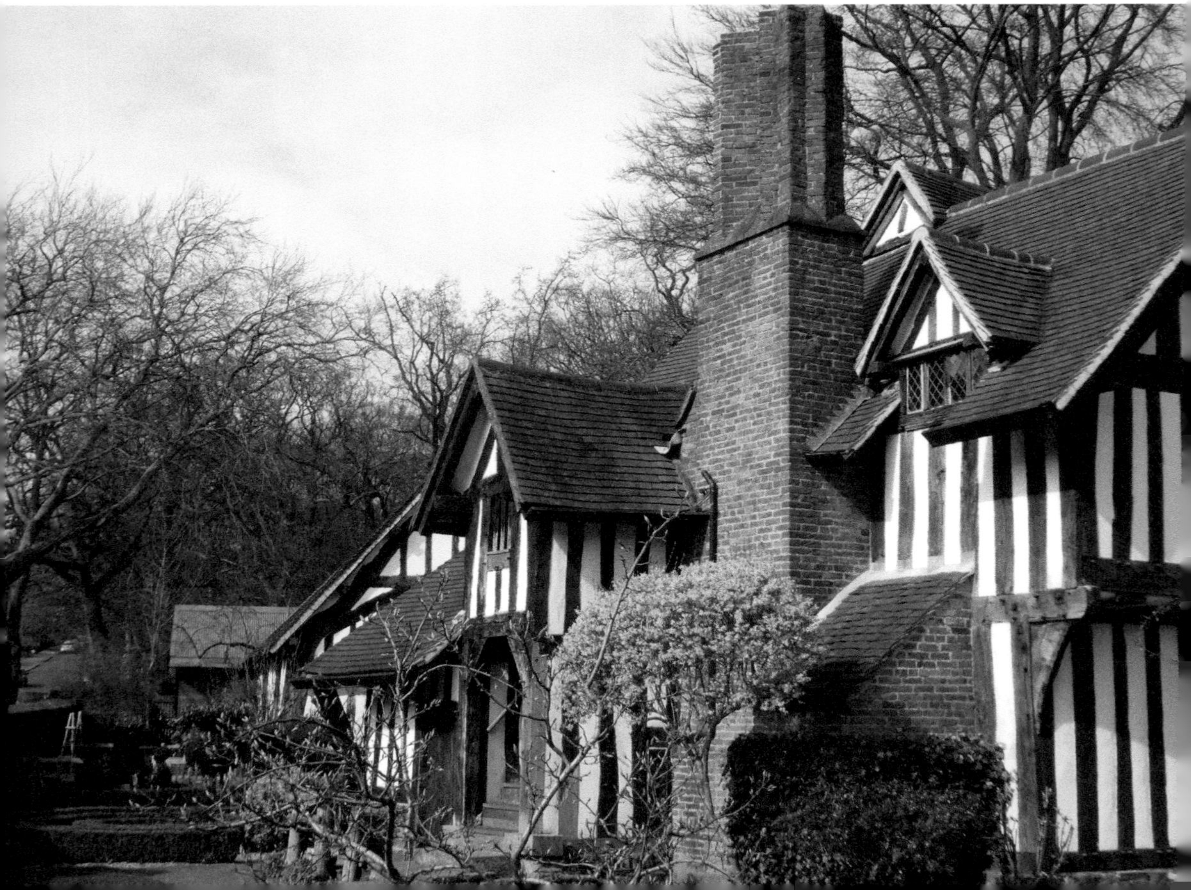

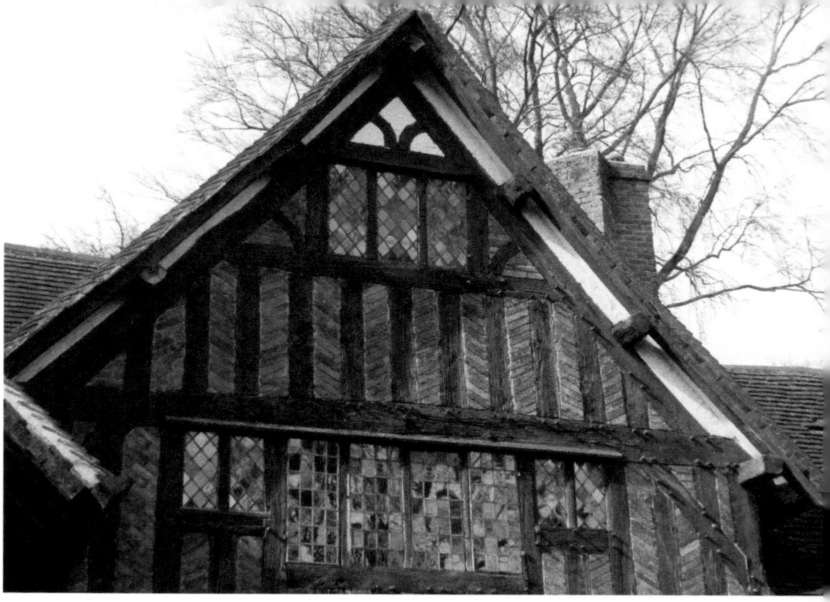

Most of the original medieval features survive intact.

The building is timber framed with plaster infill and the fifteenth-century solar wing has a jettied upper storey. The kitchen wing is timbered and dates from the early sixteenth century, while the central great hall is red brick and built in a herring bone pattern, which was painstakingly reassembled in the reconstruction. The fireplace in the great hall has tall star-shaped chimney stacks. Selly Manor has a gabled porch with low medieval doorway and casement windows with original leaded lights. Many of the original timbers have markings made by the fifteenth-century carpenters that are now on display.

3. The Old Crown (1368)

The Old Crown is in the Deritend area of Birmingham and was originally constructed by the medieval religious society the Guild of St John as their guildhall. It became an inn in the fifteenth century. The Grade II listed building has had many changes of use but still looks largely as it did when it was built in 1368.

During the English Civil War, The Old Crown was the site of a confrontation that became known as the Battle of Birmingham. The residents of Birmingham supported Cromwell and the Parliamentarians so, on Easter Monday 1643, 2,000 Royalist troops tried to storm the town. The townsfolk held them off at The Old Crown but, although they fought long and hard, the residents were eventually defeated and the Cavaliers burned and looted much of the area.

The inn survived the plunder but it gradually fell out of use and was in a state of dereliction by the nineteenth century. The Victorian parish council wanted to demolish it but it was saved by local historian and MP Joshua Smith, who bought the site and converted the building into dwellings.

In the late twentieth century the building was renovated and restored to its former use. The great hall has been converted into an array of downstairs rooms while the ancient vaulted cellars remain unchanged and are still being used for storing beer.

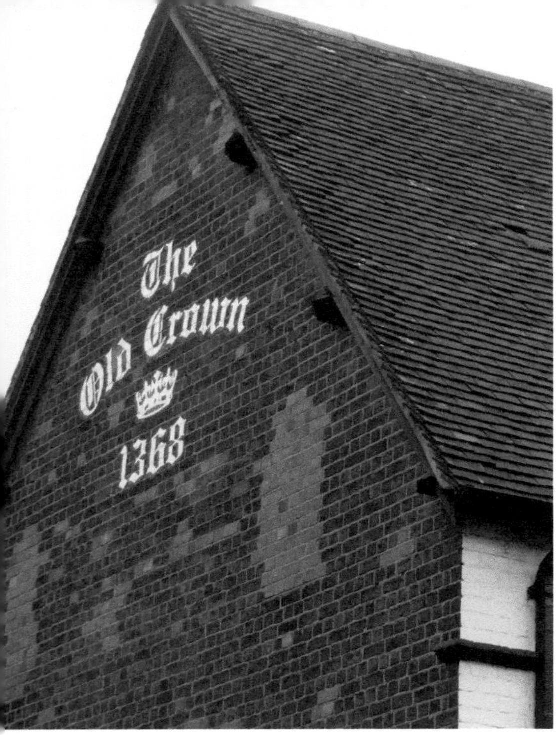

Left: The Old Crown was initially built as a guildhall.

Below: The inn retains the look of a traditional medieval building.

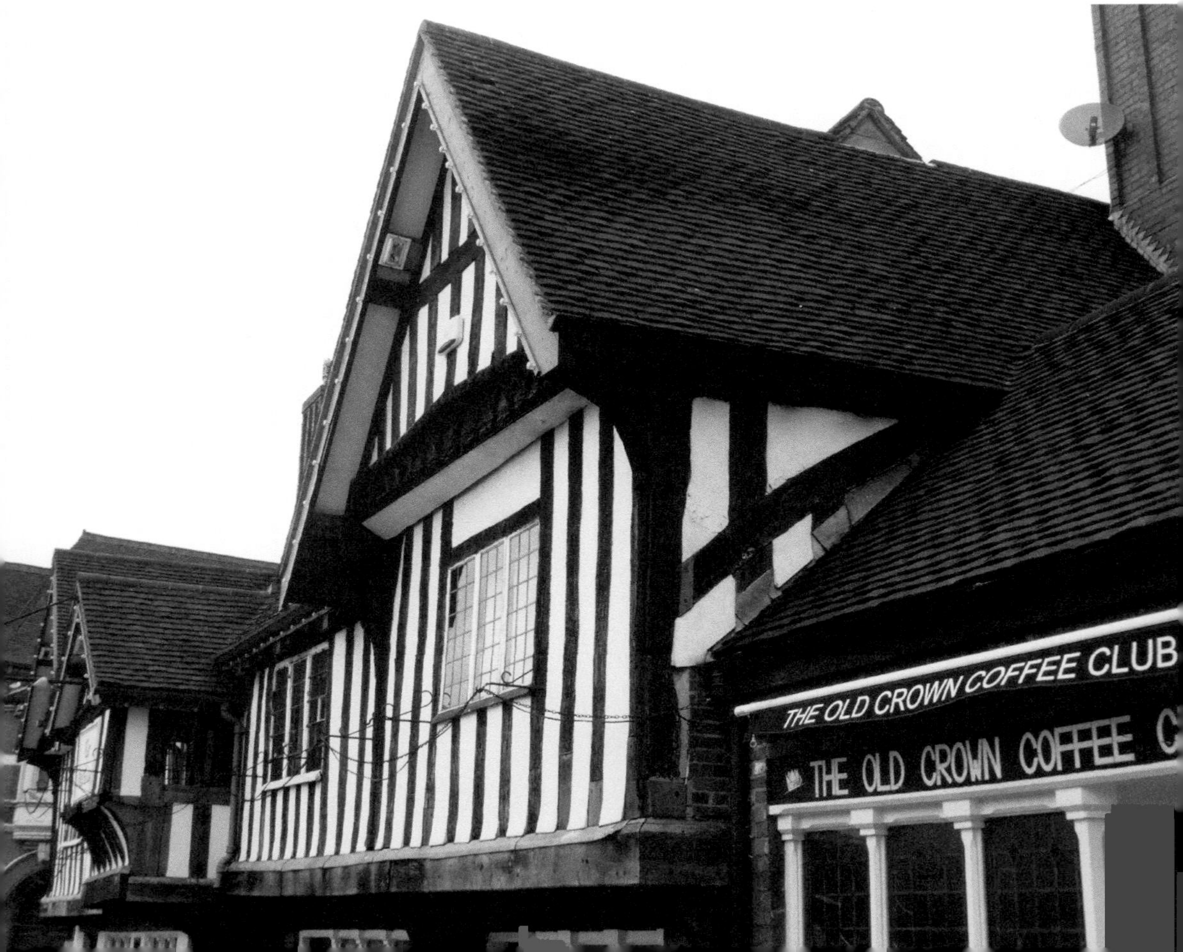

The fourteenth century builders of The Old Crown constructed it with a timber frame and plaster infill. Originally it was thatched but the pub now has a tile roof. The jettied upper floor has three dormers and the gable of the central one is above the entrance porch. All three gables have thick, elaborately carved beams that support the dormers and the property is painted in characteristic black and white.

The inn has an eleventh-century well in its beer garden. It is 40 feet deep and was unearthed during the renovations. This too has been restored.

4. The Lad in the Lane (*c.* 1400)

The Lad in the Lane in Erdington has debated with the Old Crown in Deritend for generations about which is the older establishment. Eventually, twenty-first-century dendrochronology was used to test timbers from both properties and concluded that both have fourteenth-century origins. The debate about which was built first continues.

The Lad in the Lane is a black and white timber-framed building that was originally built as a house. It is first recorded as an inn called The Green Man in the eighteenth century. Over time the name was contracted to become simply 'The Man' and it was locally known as 'The Lad'. Eventually this latter name stuck and it was officially changed to The Lad in the Lane when major alterations took place in the 1930s.

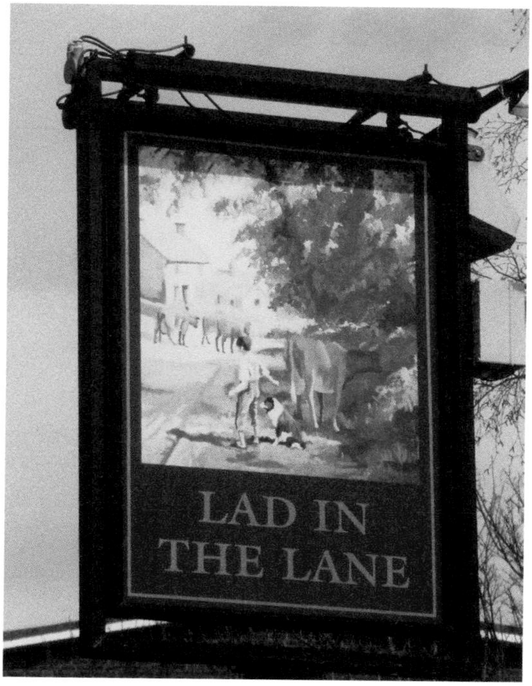

Originally called The Green Man, the pub changed name.

The L-shaped inn is Grade II listed and despite the modifications, it has retained much of its original structure. The large open-plan bar area has the original fireplace from the fourteenth-century domestic house and the 700-year-old trusses of the cruck frame are a major feature.

The 1930s extension was done sympathetically to the character of the ancient building and it is only in the greater depth of the roof and the dormer windows that the older wing of the property is revealed.

At the end of the nineteenth century, the inn was attacked by members of the infamous gang the Peaky Blinders. The Peaky Blinders were a working-class street gang involved in robbery and racketeering and they used violence to gain power within their community. Gang members wore a buttoned-down overcoat and peaked flat cap as a uniform. The name Peaky Blinder is believed to be derived from the gang's habit of stitching razor blades into the peak of their cap before headbutting opponents in the hope of blinding them.

According to reports in an 1897 local newspaper, the landlord of the inn refused to serve a group of gang members and they stoned the building in retribution. The landlord threw them out and locked all the doors but the inn came under a barrage of rocks that smashed through the windows and hit people inside, causing some serious injuries. The police arrived and arrested the gang who were subsequently charged and sentenced to a month of hard labour. The landlord immediately gave up his lease and left the area in fear of further revenge.

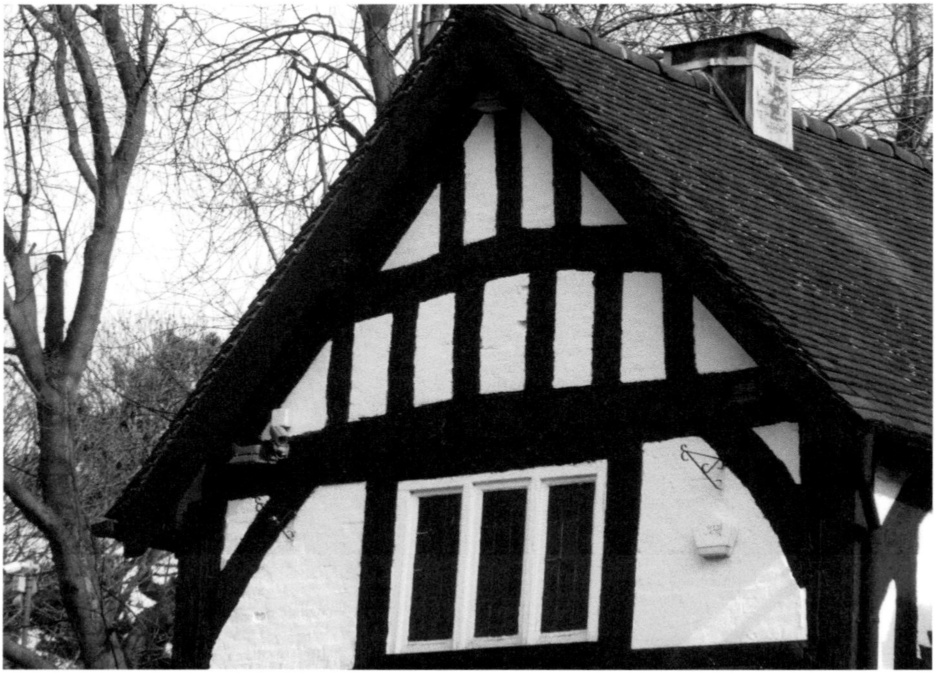

The Lad in the Lane has six centuries of history.

5. Old Grammar School (1434)

The Old Grammar School is part of a group of medieval buildings in Kings Norton. In 2004, the Grade II listed property was saved from dereliction thanks to the BBC television programme *Restoration* and a Heritage Lottery Fund grant. After extensive work, the Old Grammar School is now used as a venue for conferences and weddings.

The property was built in 1434 as a house for the priest who served the church of St Nicolas. Timbers from the largely intact structure were examined during renovation where faint carvings were discovered. These were identified as charms used in medieval houses to ward off evil spirits.

Parish records show that the house had become a school by 1547, and continued to be one until the end of the nineteenth century when it became too small for the area. During its long service as a school the property remained largely unaltered and even after it became empty the Old Grammar School retained its pleasantly old-fashioned appearance.

In 1913, the building was targeted for vandalism by the suffragette movement. The suffragettes used militant ways to promote their campaign to obtain the vote

The Old Grammar School has a picturesque setting.

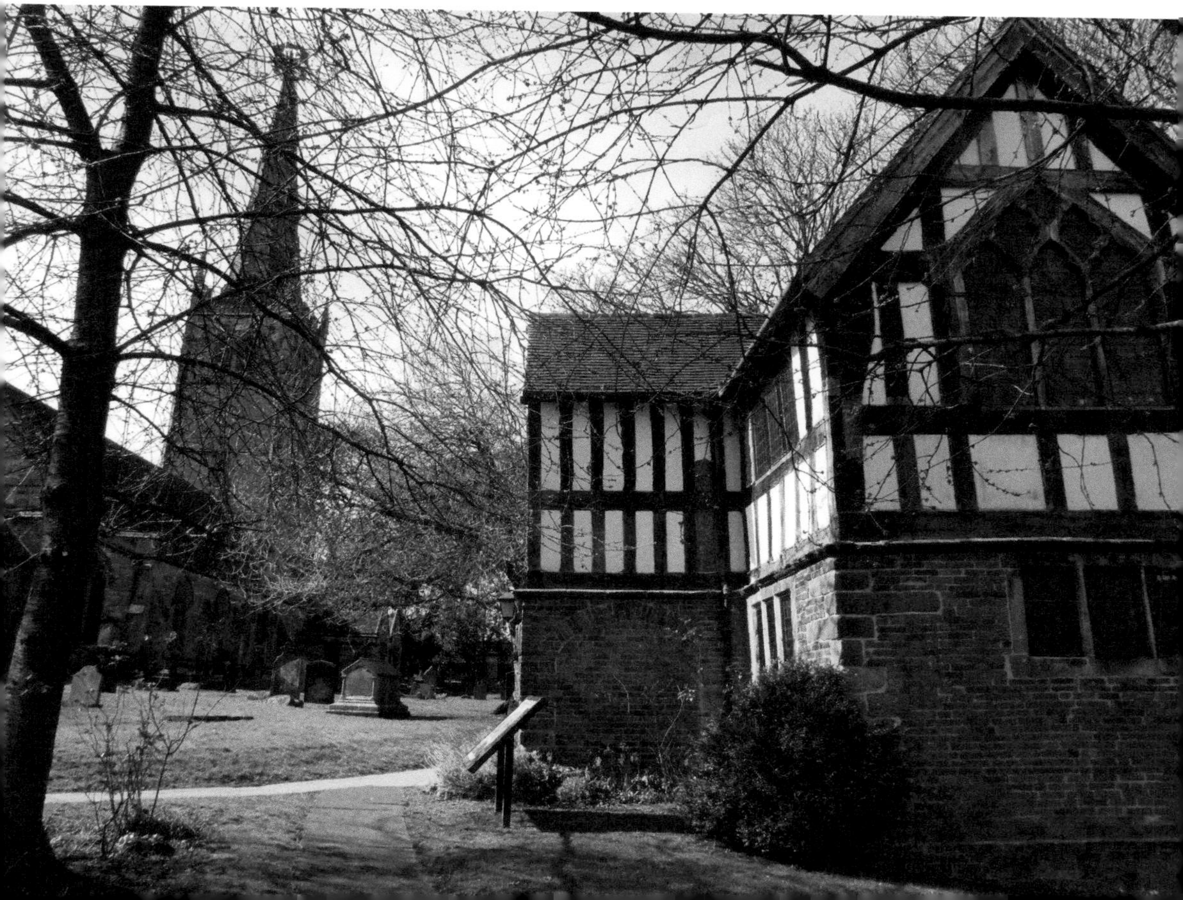

for women but they ensured there was no danger to human life. They broke into the Old Grammar School but left it untouched apart from a message written on a chalkboard that said, 'two suffragettes entered this house but were so charmed by its old-world feel that they refrained from their design of destruction.'

The charm of the Old Grammar School has been preserved to this day. The interior retains its seventeenth-century wooden panelling and original mullioned windows. These are stone framed on the ground floor, which is red brick, while the timber-framed upper storey has wooden casements. The property stands within trees on the edge of St Nicolas' churchyard and is accessed through a stone-framed door in the central gabled bay.

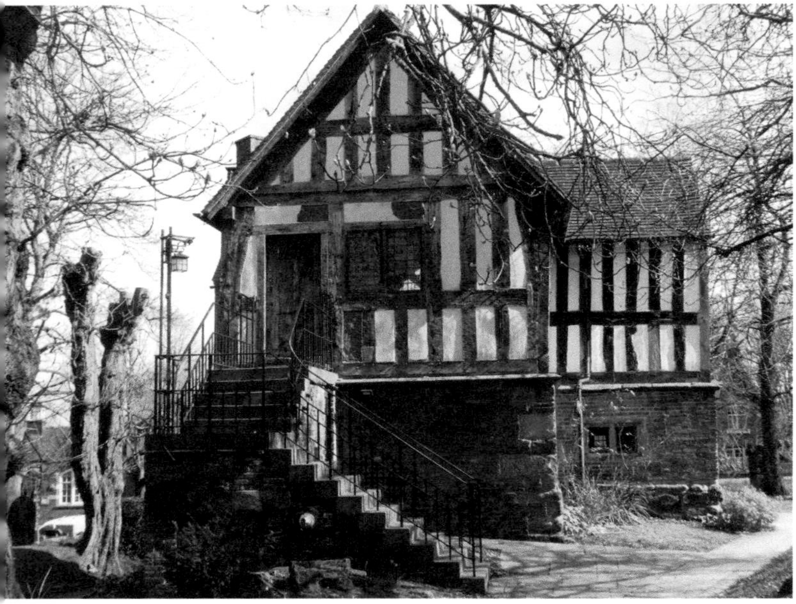

Antiquity and charm have protected the building from vandalism.

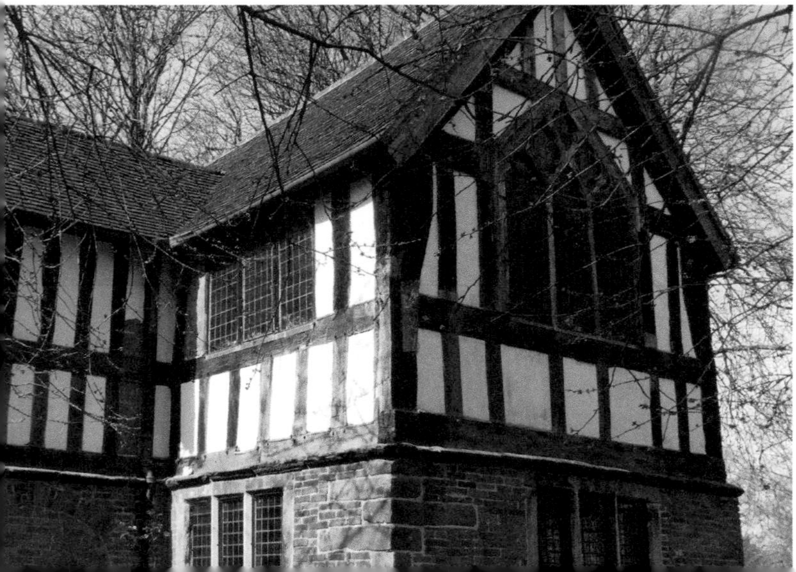

Original window frames and glass have been left in situ.

6. Tudor Merchants House (1492)

The Tudor Merchants House is in the picturesque area of Kings Norton, which has rightly been called a snapshot of the quintessential medieval English village. The property has been owned by Kings Norton parish church for some years but maintenance on the Grade II listed building was so expensive that the fifteenth-century house gradually fell into disrepair.

With the nearby Old Grammar School, it was renovated with grants provided by the television programme *Restoration* in 2004. The parish church now gets revenue for the upkeep of the building from hiring rooms within the Tudor Merchants House out for events.

The house was built for wool merchant Humphrey Rotsey in 1492 and converted into an inn during the seventeenth century. It was named The Saracens Head by its first landlord Andrew Bear and continued to trade as such for over 300 years.

Rotsey's original wooden-framed house was extended and altered but was still intact within the larger property. The solar of the original jettied house is still recognisable with its outwardly curving stud and plasterwork and original casement window.

Queen Henrietta Maria of France stayed here while taking her army to Charles I during the English Civil War and the room in which she slept bears her name.

A television programme saved the Tudor Merchants House from dereliction.

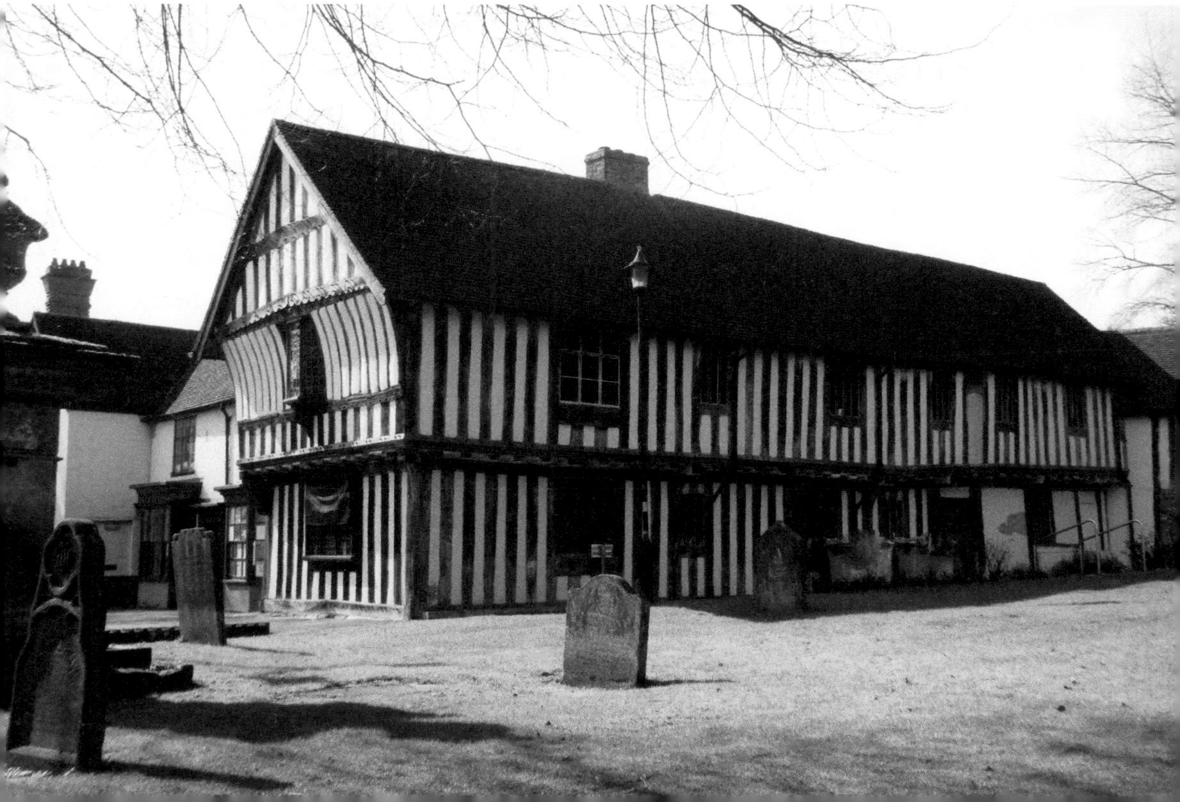

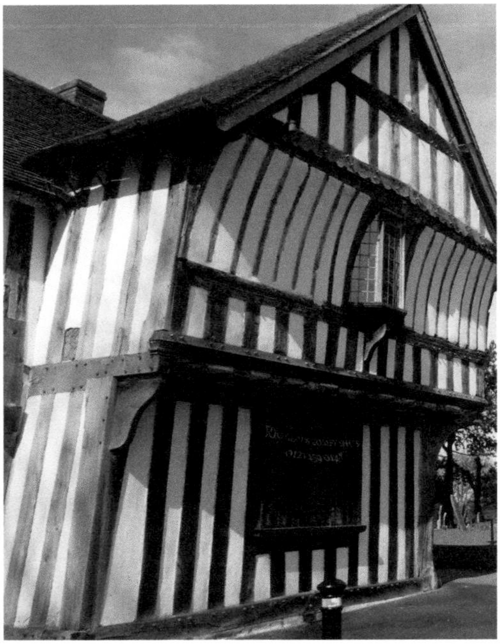
Royalty slept here during the English Civil War.

The Queens Room has an original fireplace and still retains some of the interior medieval paintwork over the wattle and daub building material.

The 2004 restoration of the Tudor Merchants House removed some later extensions and restored the domestic atmosphere of the property.

7. Blakesley Hall (1590)

Blakesley Hall is a timber-framed house in the Yardley area of Birmingham and has a Grade II listing. It has the typical dark timbering of Tudor architecture with herringbone studding and limewashed plaster. However, when it was built in 1590, this style of jettied property was already falling out of fashion. The red-brick kitchen wing at the rear of Blakesley Hall was added in 1650 and was more in keeping with subsequent Jacobean architecture.

Blakesley Hall was host to a succession of tenant farmers and it was in a dilapidated state when it was sold to Victorian businessman Henry Donne in 1899. He restored the property completely to reflect his personal perception of a sixteenth-century home. Donne was part of the Romanticism movement whose ethos was that the way of life and ideologies of the medieval period should be revived to slow down industrialisation and its associated growth in poverty and crime.

It was the Romantics who first began painting timbered properties in black and white. Tudor builders left the construction materials in their natural colours of age-darkened oak and limewashed plaster but the Victorian fashion created a starker appearance.

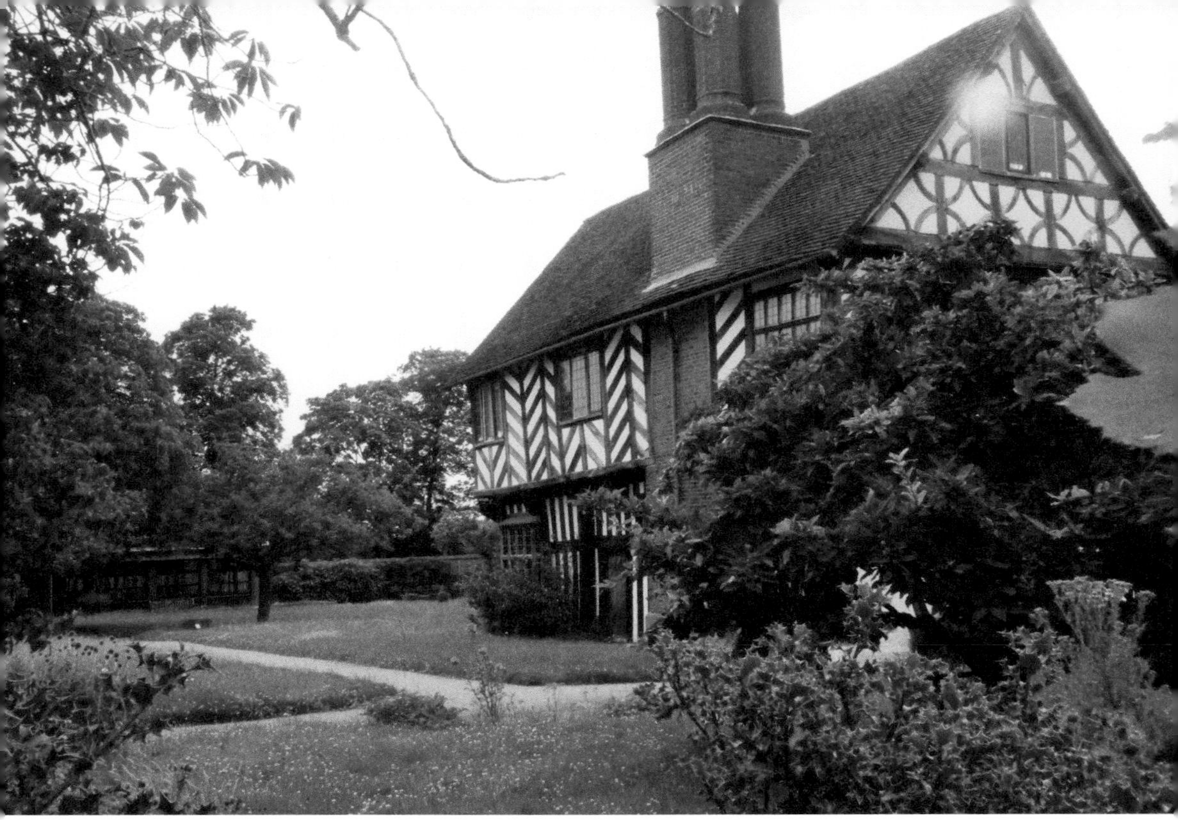

Above: Blakesley Hall shows what life was like in medieval Birmingham.

Below: Black and white timbers were the Victorian's notion of antiquity.

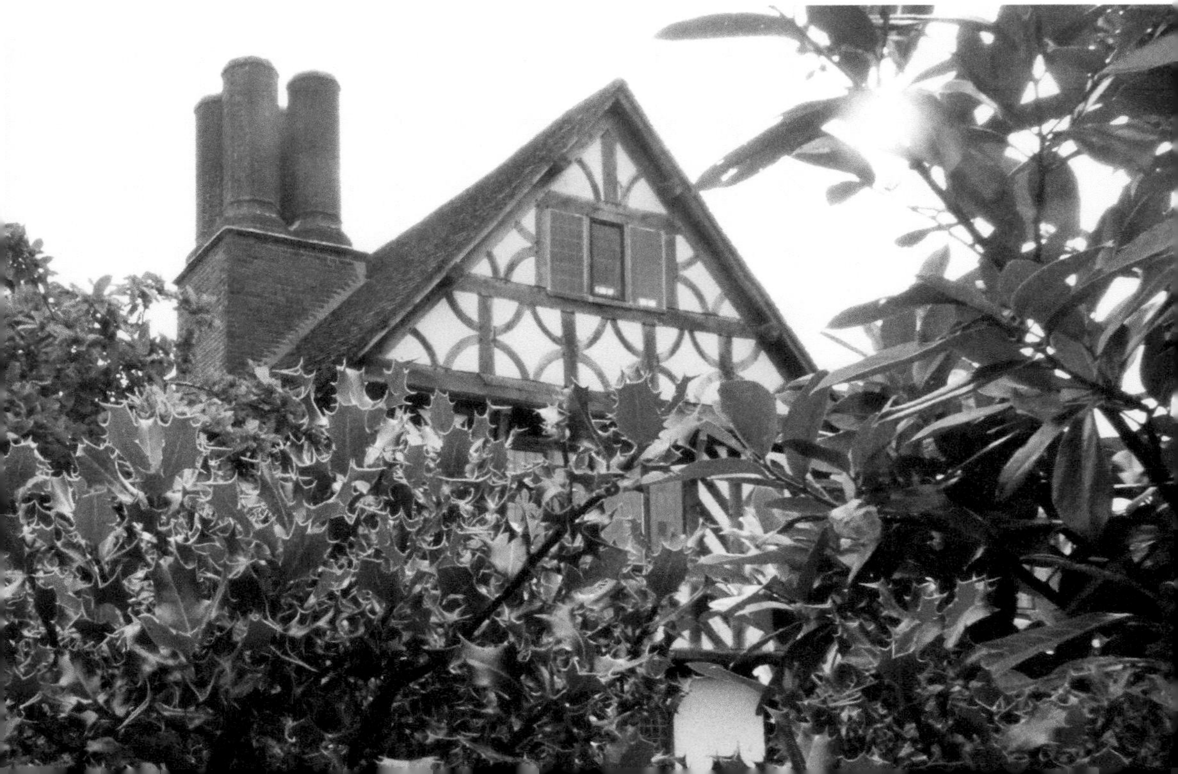

In 1941 the area around Blakesley Hall was subjected to an air raid and the hall was hit. One bomb went through the roof but fortunately it did not explode. However, there was substantial damage to the interior plasterwork and while repairing it, forgotten features were uncovered. Elizabethan candlesticks and pewter cups were discovered under floorboards in the attic and an original painted wall decoration was found where it had been plastered over in the parlour. The interior was subsequently restored to its seventeenth-century appearance and had furnishings contemporary to the era added. Since 1935 Blakesley Hall has been a museum of medieval life in the Birmingham area.

8. Aston Hall (1635)

Aston Hall was one of the last great Jacobean houses to be built in England. It was designed by architect John Thorpe for landowner Sir Thomas Holte, who moved into the completed building in 1635.

The hall, which gave its name to the Aston area of Birmingham, was built as a prodigy house. These palatial country houses were built by the wealthiest in society

Jacobean Aston Hall was designed by John Thorpe.

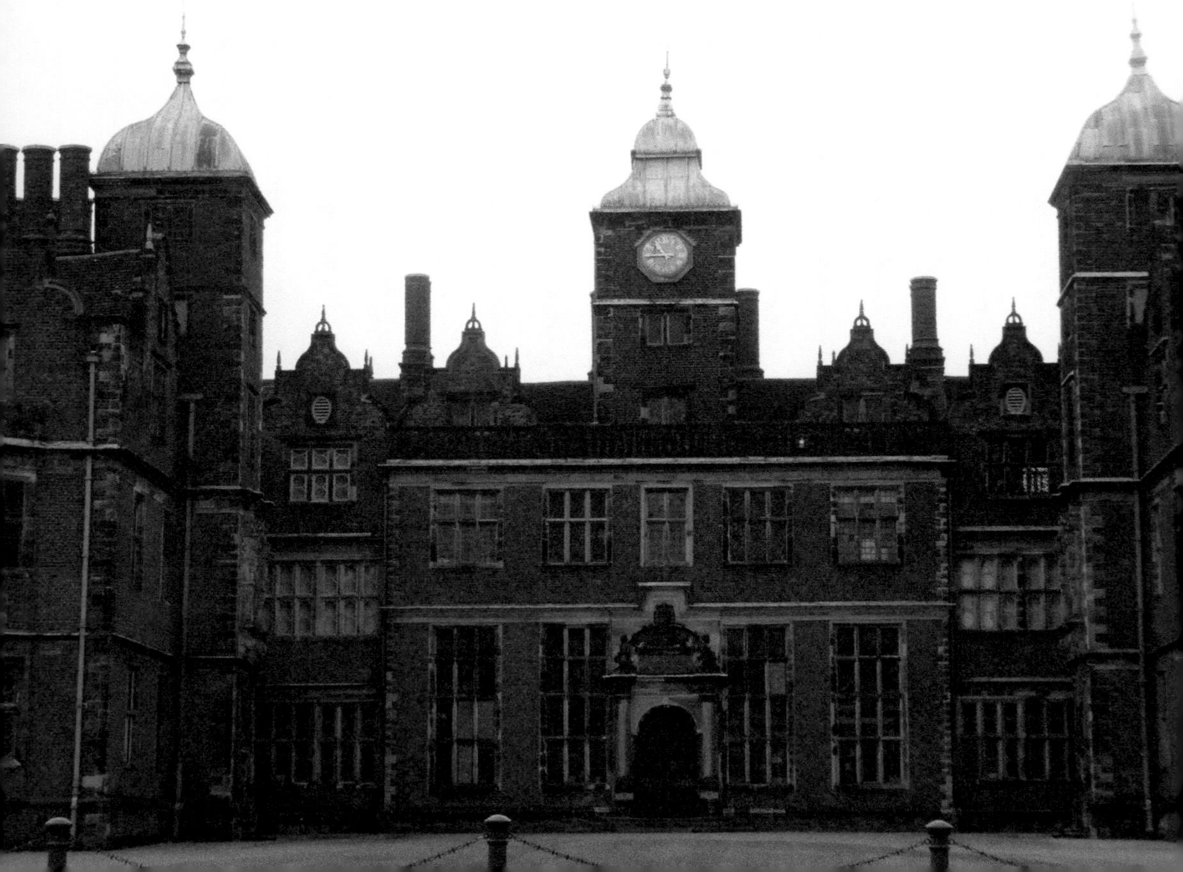

to showcase their affluence and attract elite guests. Aston Hall accommodated a king in 1643 but it created problems.

The Holte family were loyal to the crown and, on the eve of the Civil War battle of Edgehill, Charles I slept at Aston Hall. The hall was besieged by Cromwell's troops after the battle and damaged by gunfire. The great staircase has holes in the bannister where Parliamentarian cannonballs passed through the walls.

Aston Hall stayed in the Holte family until 1817 when it was sold to pay off gambling debts. It was sold to Birmingham City Council and Aston Hall became the first great house to pass into municipal ownership. The Grade I listed hall and stables have been open as a museum ever since.

The seventeenth-century Aston Hall stood within a massive hunting estate but the land has gradually been sold off to developers. The home ground of Aston Villa football club, Villa Park, now occupies land previously on Holte's estate and has a seating area named Holte's End accordingly.

The red-brick house has had very few alterations in its 400-year history. It has two forward jutting wings with curved gables and decorative semicircular crests that are characteristically seventeenth century. The central entrance is marked by three small towers capped with elegant double curve ogee turrets. Mullioned stone windows add decoration to the façade and the symmetry of the house is emphasised with the later addition of a clock face on the central tower.

The interior of the building has original wooden panelling and carved plaster ceilings. The Jacobean fireplaces are still in situ, as is the large open kitchen range.

There are many buildings on the Grade I listed site.

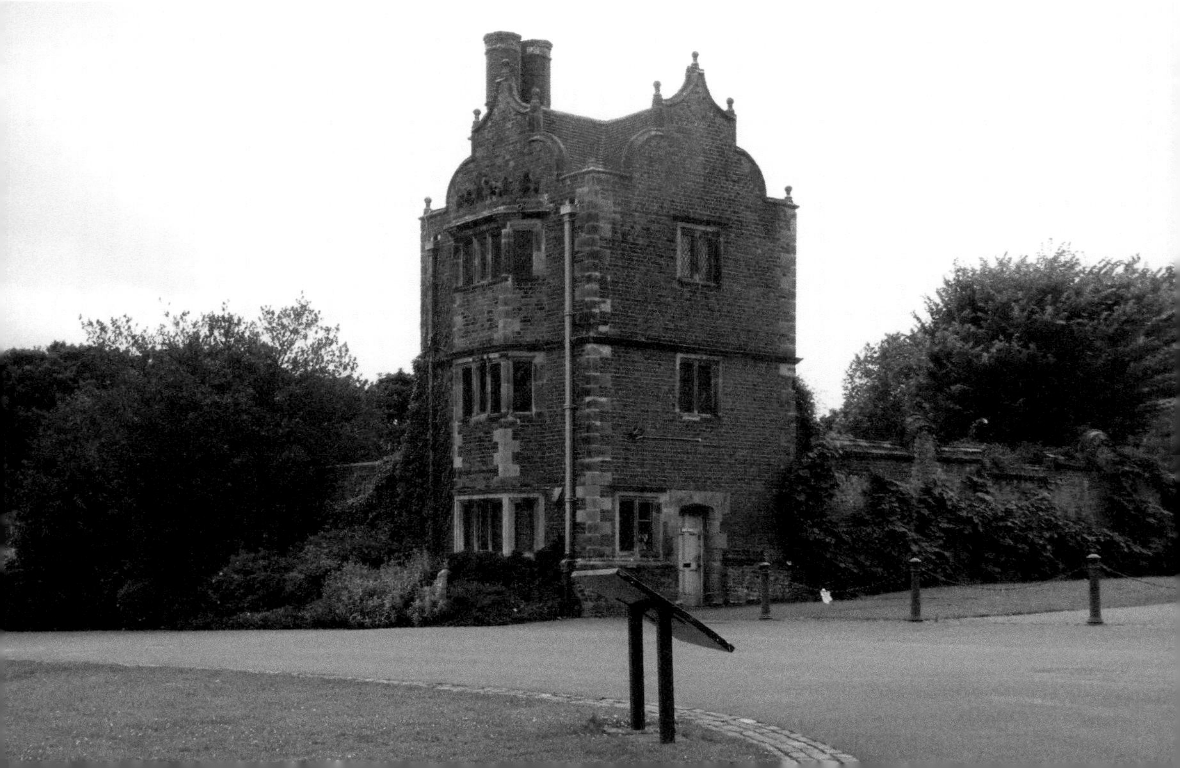

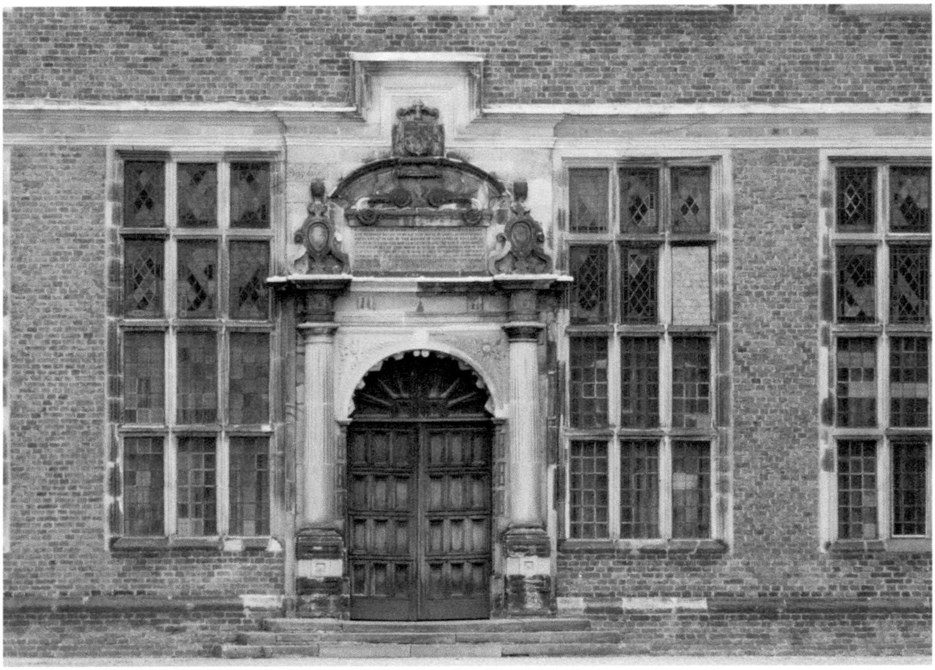

Stone detailing includes the Holte family crest.

This has an inscription above it that reminds the staff to obey the lord of the house and to remember their place as servants.

Upstairs, the long gallery stretches the length of the house and was used by residents as an exercise space when it was too inclement to walk in the grounds or ride the estate. It has a wooden floor with rush matting and the walls are lined with wall tapestries.

9. Church of the Ascension (1704)

The Church of the Ascension is a Grade II listed building in the Hall Green area of Birmingham. It was built during the reign of Queen Anne and is a fine representation of English baroque style.

The church was designed by Sutton Coldfield architect William Wilson, who had studied under Sir Christopher Wren in London. It was built using a combination of brick and stone with a stone balustrade around the slate roof. The octagonal tower at the west end has a copper cupola and it is set on each side with decorative diamond-shaped recesses. Doric pilasters and neoclassical round headed windows add further interest.

The church was originally smaller. It was built as a rectangular chapel within a walled graveyard but eventually it became too small for the growing congregation.

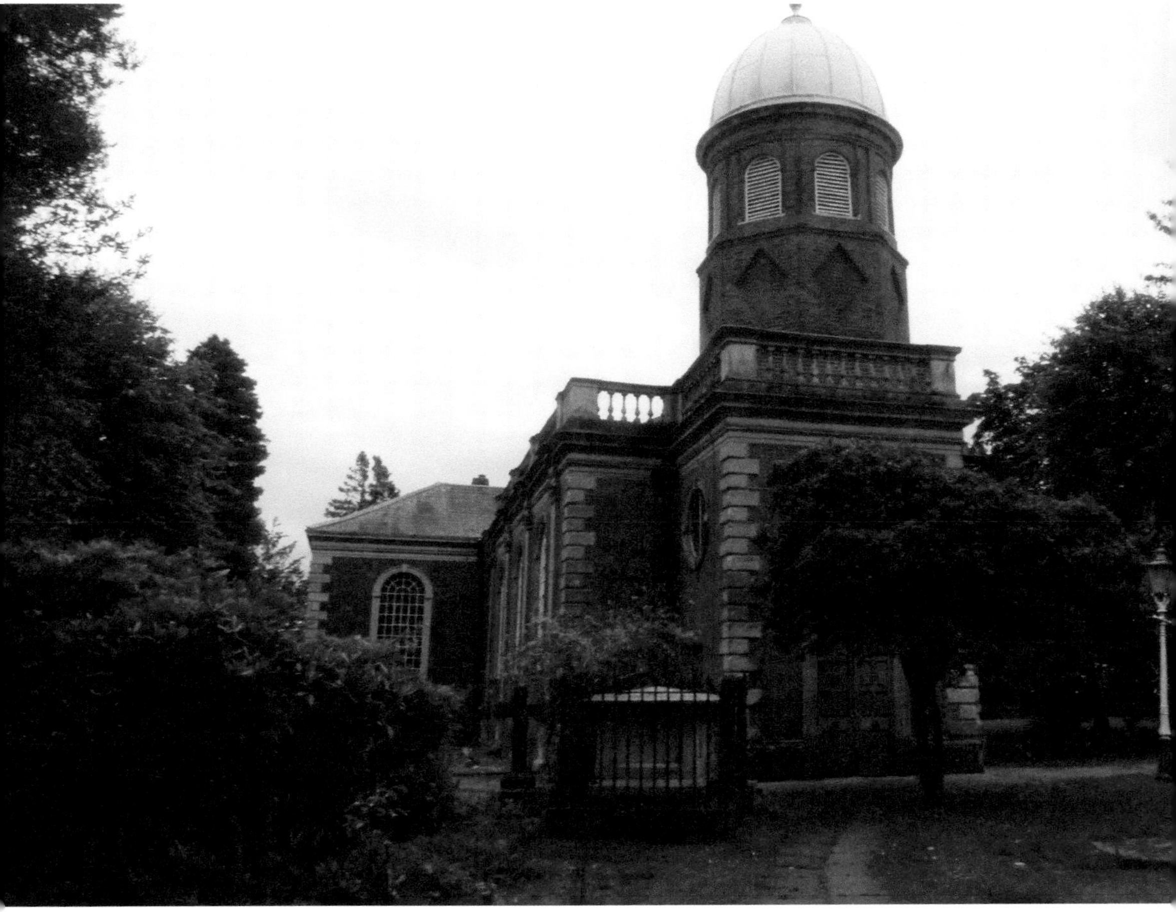

Above: Baroque architect William Wilson studied with Sir Christopher Wren.

Right: The Church of the Ascension is in an attractive setting.

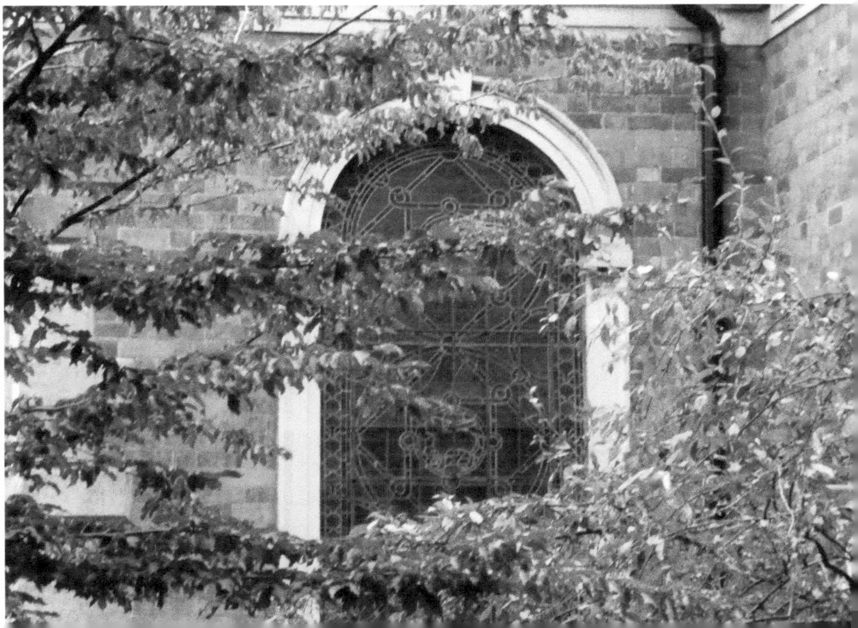

In the 1860s, the building was sympathetically enlarged with the addition of transepts and a chancel, which created a cruciform church. Architect J. G. Bland employed the English baroque style to make the alterations indistinguishable from the original.

Inside the church is a plaque dedicated to the man who originally enabled it to be built. Job Marston was a resident of Hall Green and after his death at the turn of the eighteenth century, he bequeathed a considerable amount of money to build a local place of worship. After its consecration in 1704, the church was known as Marston's Chapel. In 1954, on its 250th anniversary, it was rededicated as the Church of the Ascension.

A sign displayed in the church concerns the old practice called the disposal of seats. It lists all of the pews and the name of the family permitted to use them. Wealthy families would rent or buy pews for Sunday worship and it was a status symbol to be closest to the front.

10. St Philip's Cathedral (1715)

St Philip's is one of the smallest Anglican cathedrals in the country. It was built in 1715 and was designed by Thomas Archer, the architect to Queen Anne. Archer was a leader in the English baroque style and his work is so highly decorative that it has been described as being virtually theatrical. Historic England have granted St Philip's a Grade I listing and they refer to it as a rare and very fine example of its genre.

When building began on St Philip's in 1711, Birmingham was still a fairly small town and the design was unusually grand. However, during the eighteenth century the population of Birmingham increased 900 per cent and the town grew around St Philip's. It became the heart of fashionable Georgian life.

St Philip's had been designed to be just a parish church. However, when Birmingham was granted city status by Queen Victoria in 1889, the decision was taken not to build a new place of worship but to make the resplendent St Philip's into the cathedral. The rectangular footprint of the church was altered by adding an arched chancel and the exterior stone was refaced. The church had been built in brick with a limestone facing but this proved to be too fragile for the industrial environment of the town and had begun to crumble away. Major repairs to the façade were completed in readiness for its new position as a cathedral.

St Philip's tower exemplifies the church's Italianate style with a dome surmounted by a lantern. A stone balustrade around the leaded roof is set with decorative urns and the stone pilasters, which separate the arched windows, following classical design.

The church was completely fitted out in timber and while two of the galleries are still in place, the box pews and three-tier pulpit have since been removed. Parts of the original 1715 wooden organ also exist, although the instrument has been moved to a new position and has been substantially repaired.

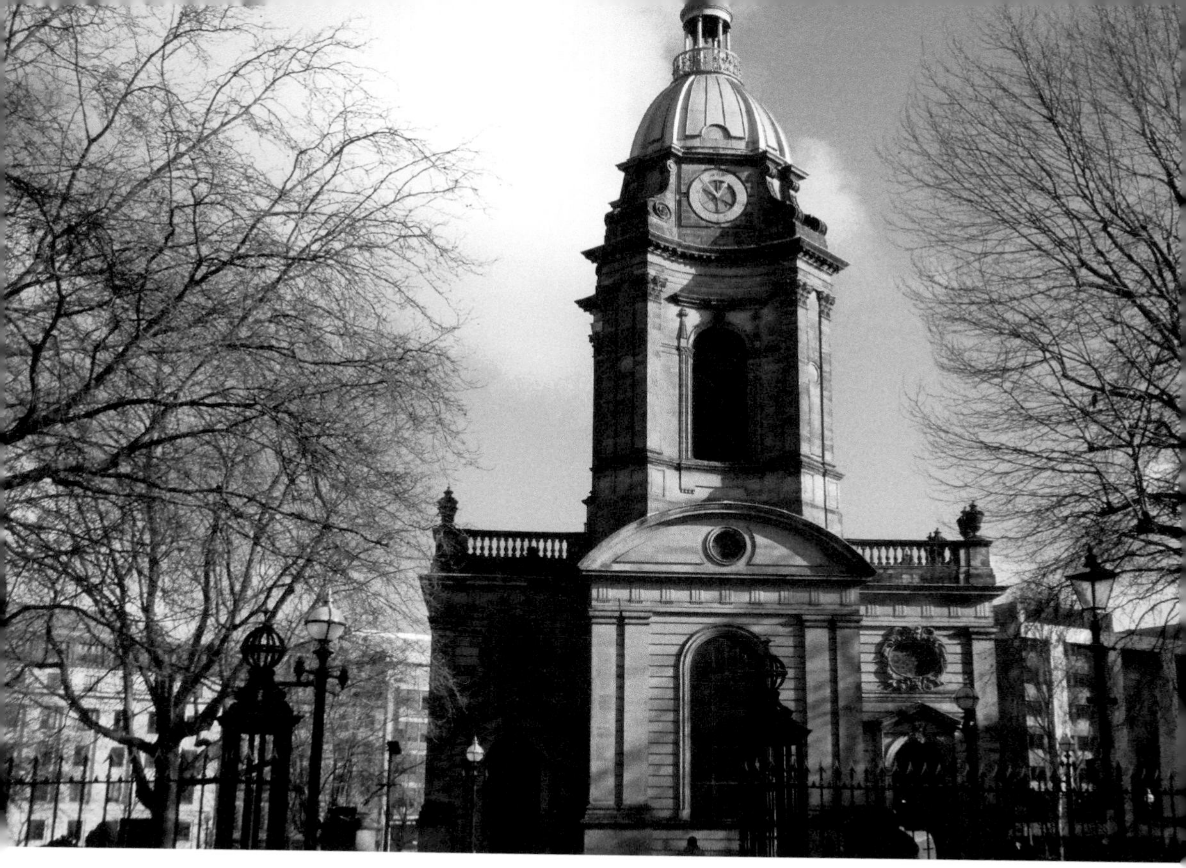

Above: St Philip's is a small but highly decorative cathedral.

Right: The Italianate clock tower has a lead dome.

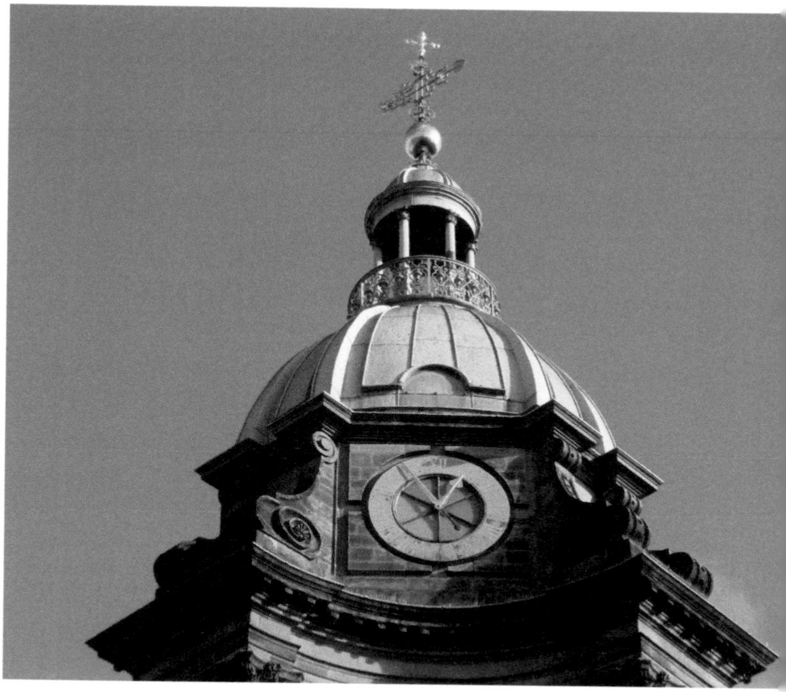

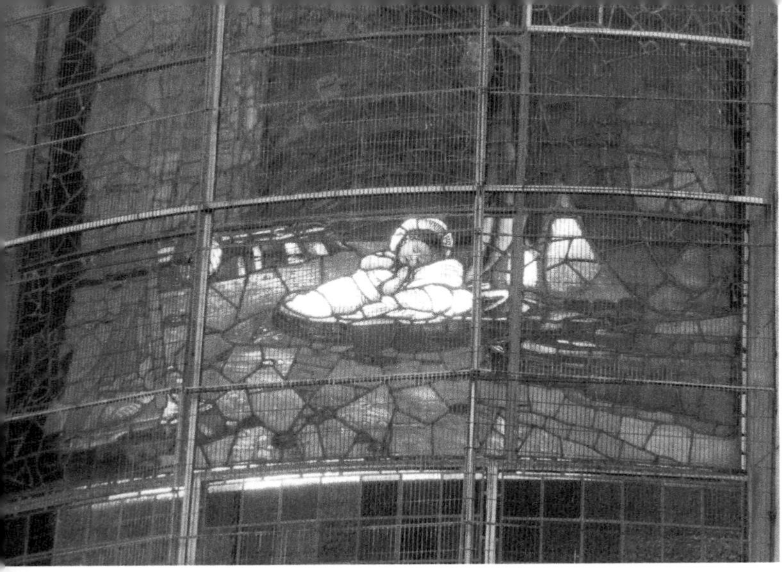

Edward Burne-Jones designed some of the priceless windows.

In 1940 the cathedral was hit during an air raid and left badly damaged. The stained glass had been removed to storage at the outbreak of the Second World War and was returned intact to St Philip's after its repair and reopening in 1948. The stained glass includes four priceless windows designed by Edward Burne-Jones, who was born in the parish of St Philip's and had been christened in the church. They were made by the leading manufacturer of the Arts and Crafts movement, Morris and Co.

11. Perrott's Folly (1758)

John Perrott was the owner of a large Georgian house and hunting estate in the eighteenth century. The estate has since been developed into the residential area of Rotton Park and the house was demolished. However, the folly that Perrott built for himself still towers above the surrounding modern houses.

The 100-foot red-brick tower was built in 1758. Some people believe that it was only intended to be an ostentatious statement, while sentimentalists suggest that John Perrott had it constructed to be able to see the grave of his wife, who was buried 15 miles away, from the top. However, it is possible that the tower was used by Perrott to entertain his peers while watching hunting on the estate. Perrott and his guests would have been able to see the whole estate from the top in fine weather or from one of the rooms below if wet. The interior rooms all have elaborate plasterwork decorations and large arched windows, which suggests that they were designed to receive and impress guests.

After the estate was sold in the late nineteenth century, the hexagonal tower was used as a weather recording station until the site moved to the campus of the University of Birmingham in 1979.

Perrott's Folly gained a Grade II listing from Historic England, although it was on their list of buildings at risk and it took thirty years to raise funds to make the structure safe and enable public access. The Gothic tower now hosts charity art

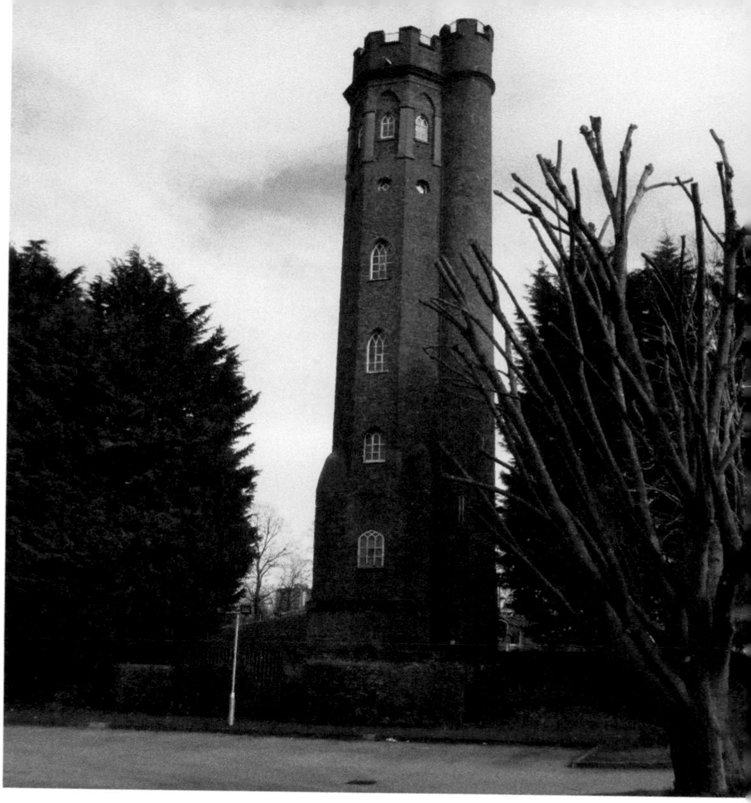

There are many suggestions about the purpose of the tower.

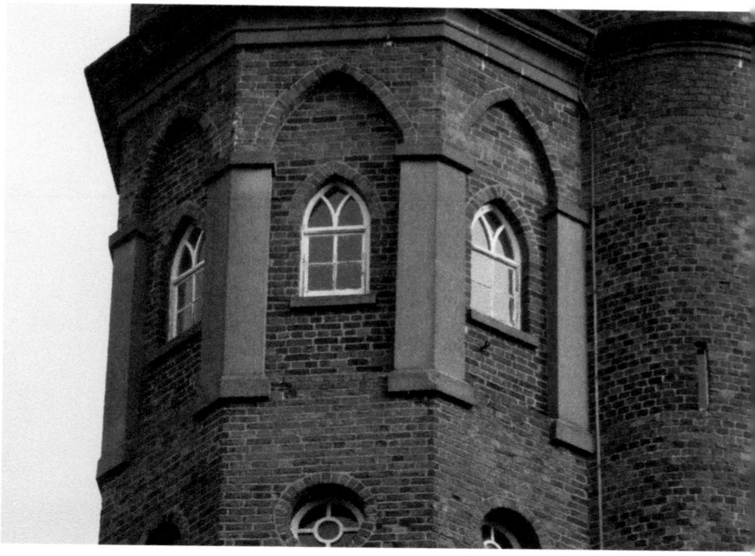

Perrott's Folly was an inspiration for author J. R. R. Tolkien.

events and it is occasionally opened for those who wish to climb the 139 steps to the top and be rewarded with outstanding views.

The structure also features as a destination on the Tolkien Trail, an unofficial route around Birmingham visiting sites that inspired the author J. R. R. Tolkien. The writer lived nearby when he was young and Perrott's Folly was the inspiration for the brooding Orthanc Tower in *The Lord of the Rings*.

12. Soho House (c. 1760)

Soho House is a classic Georgian building. It contains a museum exploring the life of Industrial Revolution pioneer Matthew Boulton, who was born in Birmingham and lived in Soho House for much of his life. Boulton was at the forefront of scientific and industrial discoveries. He co-invented the steam engine with James Watt, which led to mechanised manufacturing and mass production.

Matthew Boulton bought the land on which the house stands in 1766. The area is now part of Handsworth, but then it was a large rural estate with properties on it including a mill and a new but unfinished cottage. Boulton employed architect Samuel Wyatt, who was a leader in the neoclassical style, to develop the cottage into Soho House where he lived until his death in 1809. The mill became the Soho Manufactory, the first factory that mass-produced goods on an assembly line. After the estate passed out of the hands of the Boulton family in the 1850s, the manufactory was demolished.

Soho House was used as a hotel before it was bought by Birmingham City Council and turned into a museum in 1990. Inside the museum are many items that were made in the manufactory in the eighteenth and nineteenth centuries. These include silver work and items decorated in ormolu, which was a method of plating bronze in gold. The interior of the house has been restored to reflect its Georgian origins. Matthew Boulton was forward thinking and innovative and when he moved into the house, he installed a central-heating system, heated bath and indoor flushing toilet, all of which were unknown at that time.

The property is white painted and symmetrical in design and has a Grade II listing from Historic England. It is brick built, although it appears to be stone due to a cladding of large slate tiles. The house has three storeys of windows for natural light and they also add interest to the façade, alongside the decorated full-height Ionic pilasters. There are deep bay windows to the side and rear, which used to face on to the extensive gardens. The land was sold off for building in the twentieth century.

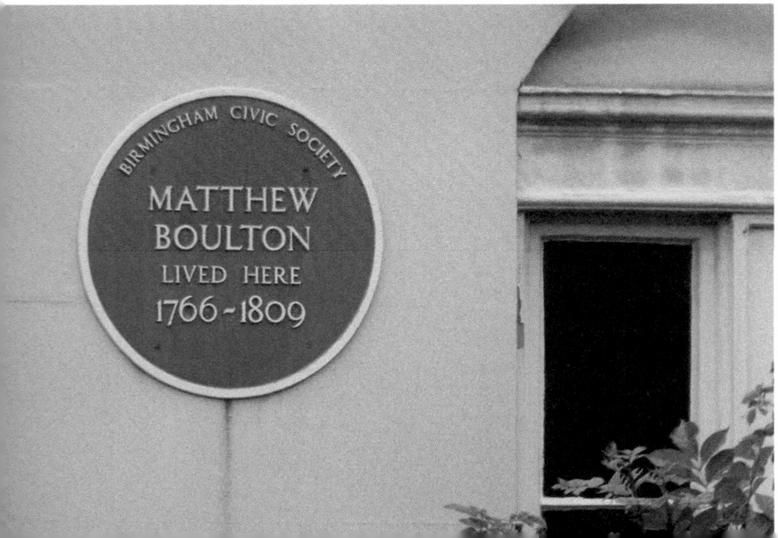

Birmingham-born Matthew Boulton was an industrialist and inventor.

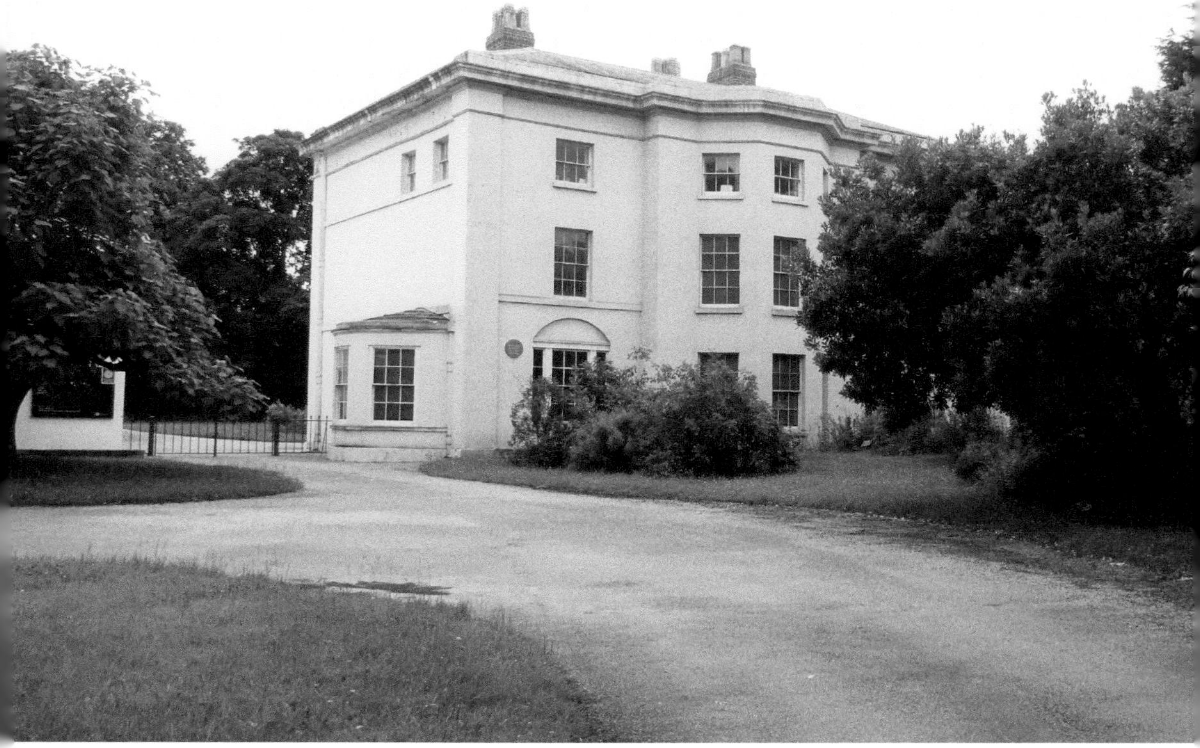

Modern amenities were built into the Georgian house.

13. Sarehole Mill (1768)

There has been a watermill on this site in Hall Green since the fourteenth century and this original Tudor structure was bought by Matthew Boulton in the eighteenth century.

The industrialist completely rebuilt the property in 1768 to convert Sarehole Mill from flour production into a site for the manufacturing of rolled sheet metal for buttons. Sarehole Mill has remained largely unchanged since then and has been restored to house a popular working museum attracting 18,000 visitors each year.

The Grade II listed mill has a very characteristic profile due to the tall, slender chimney that gives it an industrial appearance and was added when a steam engine was installed. The engine was used when water levels were too low for the waterwheel to function properly and Sarehole had the most constant production rate of the fifty other mills on the River Cole at that time.

Sarehole Mill was used until 1919 after which, although it was occupied, it gradually fell into disrepair. When the final occupant died in 1959 it became the target for vandals who nearly destroyed it. The local community and author J. R. R. Tolkien mounted campaigns to save it from demolition.

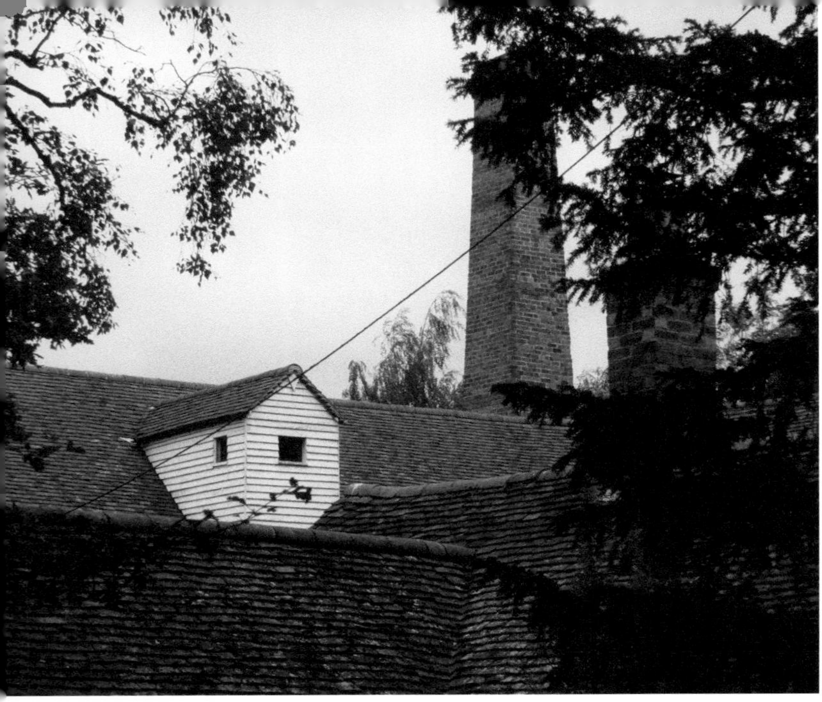

Left: Picturesque Sarehole Mill was used for the manufacture of metal.

Below: Author J. R. R. Tolkien helped to save the mill from demolition.

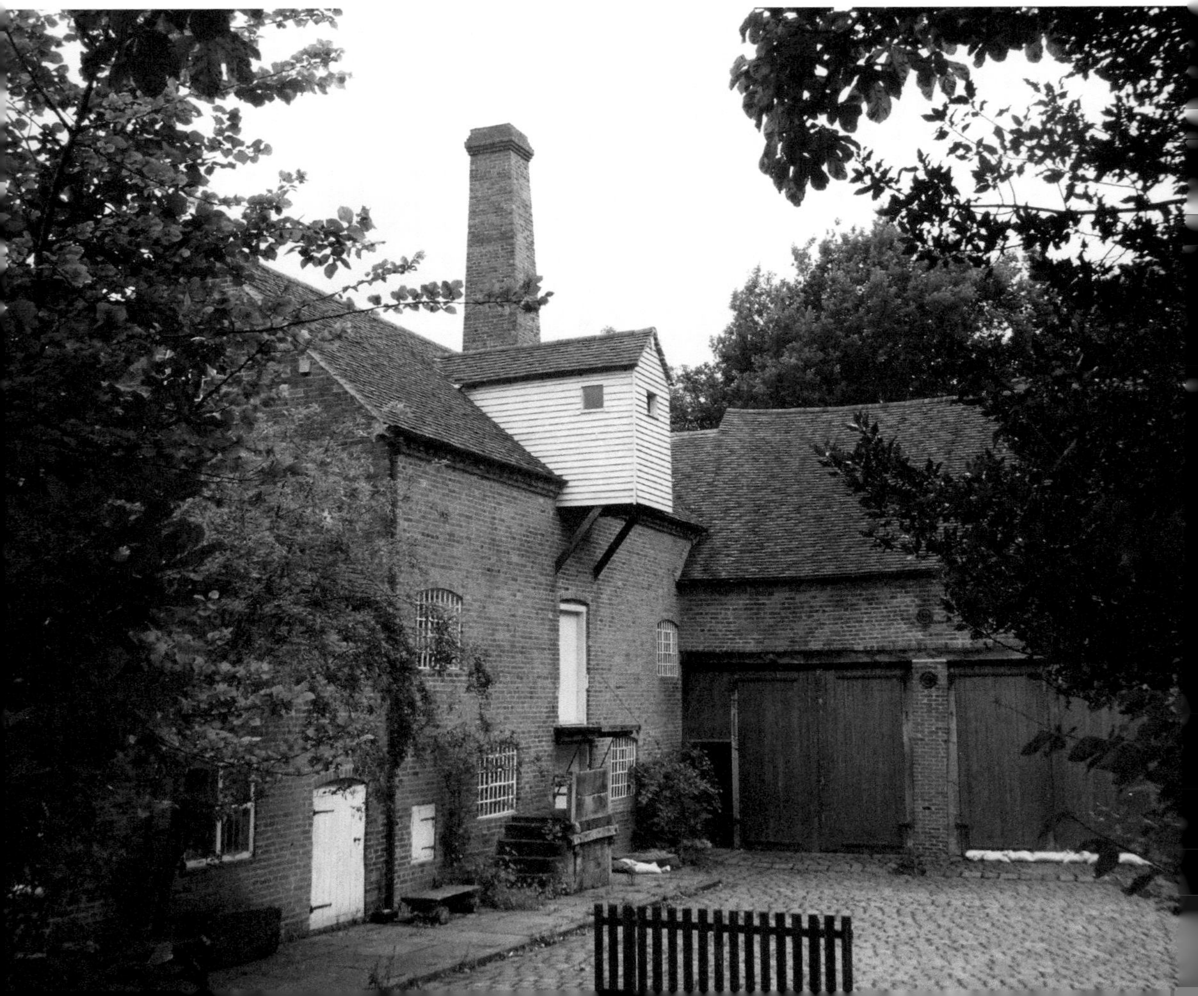

Tolkien had moved to a cottage opposite Sarehole Mill in 1896 when he was four years old. The area had a great impact on him and the watermill inspired him in his writings. It became a model for some of the settings in *The Lord of the Rings*.

The campaigns saved the mill from demolition and it was completely restored in 1969 to its eighteenth-century appearance. Sarehole Mill is brick built throughout with a tiled roof and iron-framed windows. Many of the original millstones and gears are still operational, as is the white weatherboard hoist used for easy management of goods and produce. The whole area is now a pilgrimage for fans of Tolkien and his works.

14. St Paul's Church (1779)

St Paul's Church has understated Georgian simplicity. It is in the Jewellery Quarter of Birmingham, surrounded by the town houses built for wealthy jewellers who arrived in the area soon after the church's consecration in 1779. Grade I listed St Paul's has become known as the Jeweller's Church for this reason.

St Paul's was frequented by those in the jewellery trade.

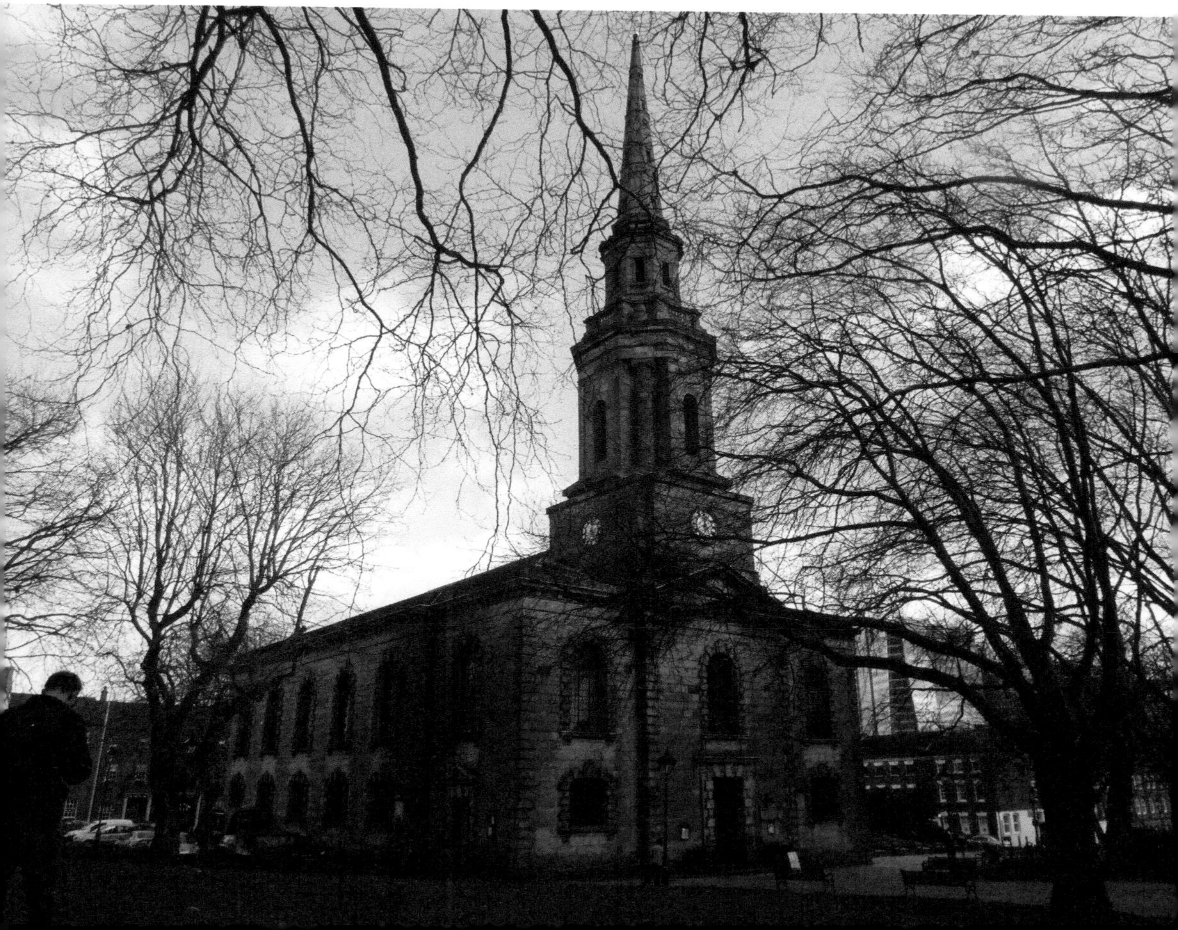

The Jewellery Quarter has been home to Europe's greatest concentration of jewellery businesses for 250 years. Craftsmen were so proud of their skills that their apprentices were expected to gain qualifications from the Birmingham School of Art before starting work. Although the industry has declined during the twenty-first century, local businesses still produce 40 per cent of British jewellery.

Industrialist Matthew Boulton worshipped at St Paul's where he had a private box pew. All of the original wooden pews still remain in the church and the interior is largely as it was in Boulton's time.

Marble tablets decorate the walls which were all made by Birmingham's William Hollins, a leading sculptor of the Georgian era to whom one of the stained-glass windows was made as a memorial. Much of the other stained glass is late Victorian, except for the east window, which is the masterpiece of the church. It is an eighteenth-century artwork in painted glass and enamel created by Francis Eginton, an extraordinary glass designer who based his design for *The Conversion of St Paul* on a painting of the same name.

St Paul's Church was designed by architect Roger Eykins. It is built using ashlar and has a simple tiled roof. On completion of the church, Eykins has not managed to realise his vision for a spire and the church was left with a simple tower until the octagonal lantern and steeple were added in 1823. Bomb damage in the Second World War claimed the original roof of the church, but fortunately the tower escaped undamaged.

St Paul's is often described as an oasis of calm in the city centre and visitors sit in the grassy square enjoying the peaceful atmosphere the place of worship evokes.

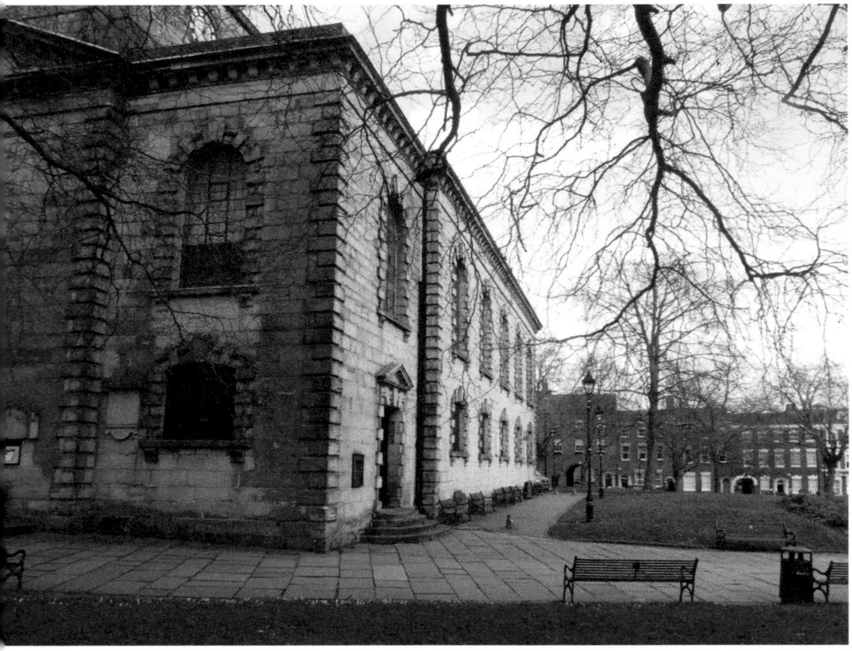

The Georgian church has classical simplicity.

15. Birmingham Gun Barrel Proof House (1813)

Gun making was an important part in the manufacturing history of Birmingham. In the nineteenth century nearly half of the world's guns were produced in the small area of Birmingham known as the Gun Quarter.

Birmingham was the centre of the worldwide gun trade and part of the area's heritage which survives is the Grade II listed Gun Barrel Proof House on Banbury Street. The building is still a vital part of England's gun industry as it is used to ensure the safety of firearms. Every gun has to be tested and stamped to show it is safe to use. This is achieved by loading an overcharged cartridge into the weapon and firing it to prove the barrel can withstand far more explosive pressure than it would normally have to deal with. It was the gun manufacturers of Birmingham who petitioned parliament to make safety testing a legal requirement and the Birmingham Gun Barrel Proof House was built in 1813 to do the necessary assessments.

The building was designed by local architect and builder John Horton in the Tuscan style. It surrounds a cobbled courtyard with covered walkways to enable movement from one part of the building to another, and entrance to the complex is through an arched gateway. The Proof House is a two-storey red-brick property decorated with painted stonework and terracotta. The neoclassical arched windows have subtle pediments and the main door has Italianate pilasters on either side. Over the door is an elaborately coloured coat of arms and above this is a simple clock face.

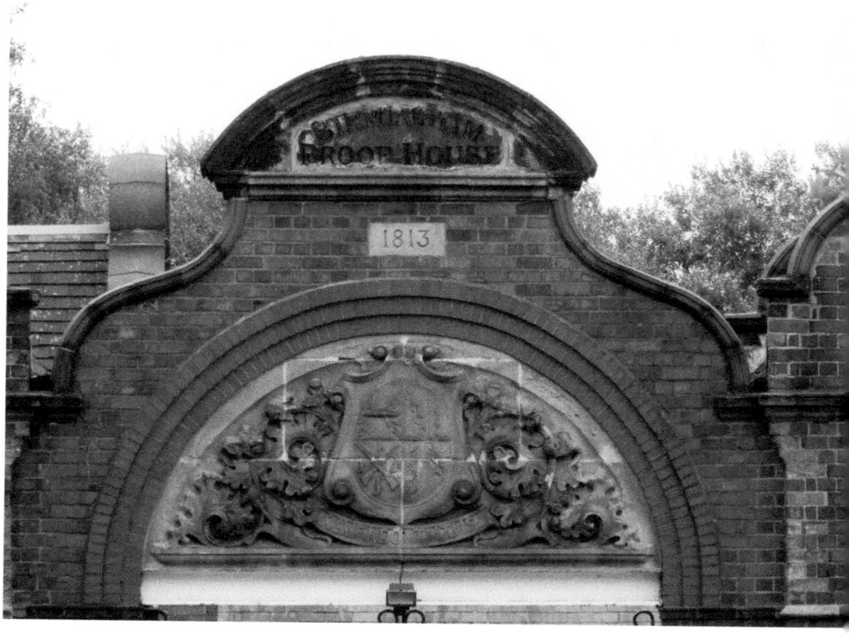

Birmingham Gun Barrel Proof House still tests firearm safety.

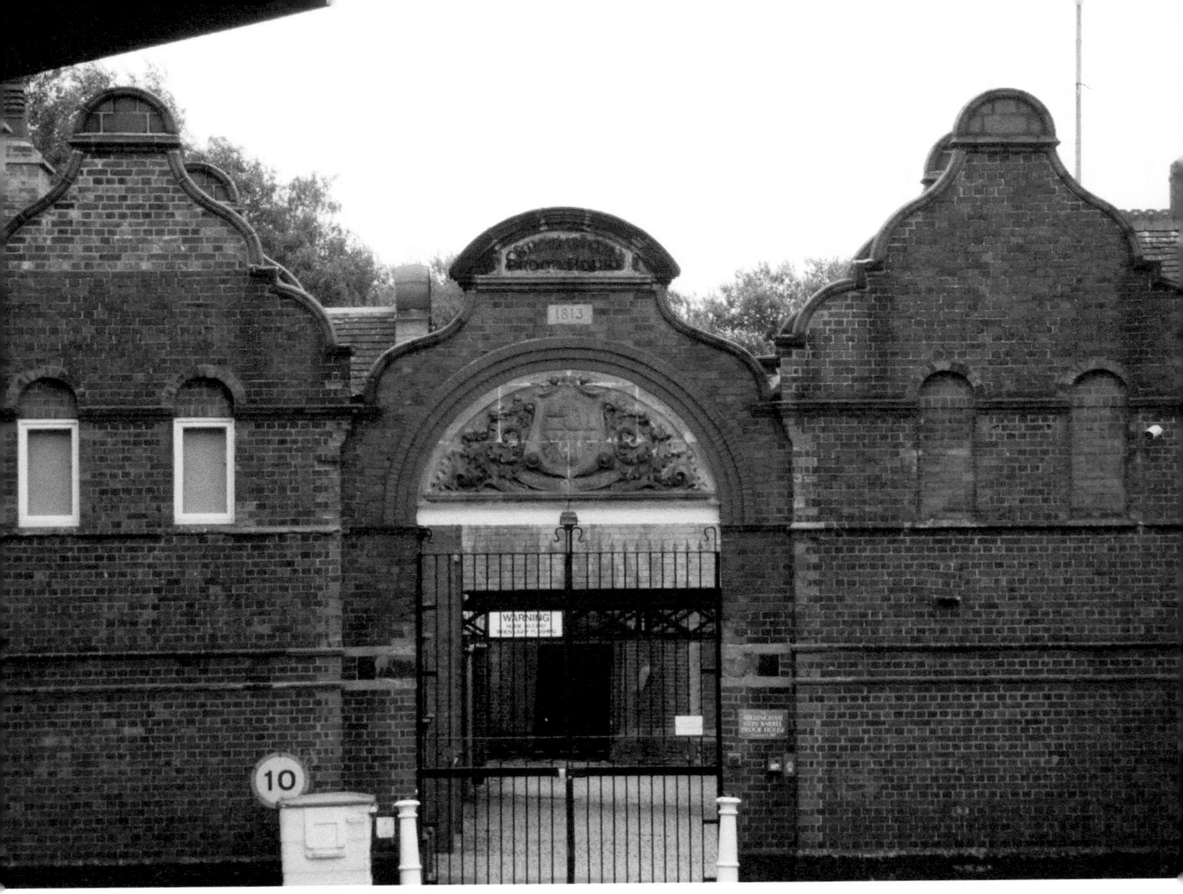

Local architect John Horton designed the elaborate gable ends.

The Birmingham Gun Barrel Proof House has remained in use for two centuries and is largely unchanged. Original features include the external rainwater spouts, an original interior in one of the boardrooms on the upper floor and the proof hole. This is where the test firing of guns takes place. The proof hole was hit with a bomb in 1940 but, due to it being constructed to withstand the discharging of weapons, it sustained little damage.

The Proof House has a small museum dedicated to items associated with the manufacture of small arms and ammunition and has records relating to proof testing and how it links to the industrial past of Birmingham.

16. Kings Norton Stop Lock (1814)

Kings Norton has the only guillotine-gated lock in Great Britain and it is a unique part of canal navigation history. Kings Norton Stop Lock is at the junction of the Stratford upon Avon and the Worcester and Birmingham canals and was constructed in 1814. It has a Grade II listing from Historic England due to its uniqueness.

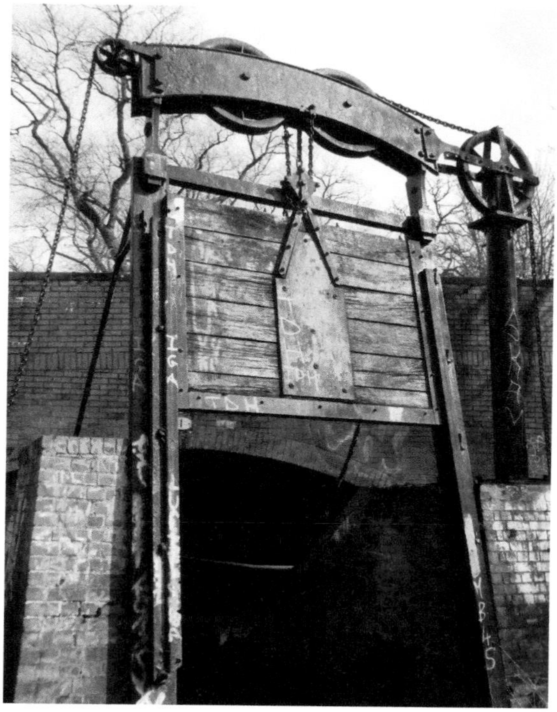

Kings Norton guillotine gated lock is unique on British waterways.

The stop lock consists of a brick-lined chamber. A cast-iron frame supports the mechanism that lifts the wooden gates at each end of the pound. The gate was designed to be hoisted up and down vertically as it took up less room than traditional gates, which needed to be pushed open by hand using the balance bar after draining the lock. Kings Norton lock did not need a lock key to equalise the water levels as there was only a 6-inch difference between the two pounds. Since it was restored in 2013, the gates of the lock are left permanently open.

In the sixteenth and seventeenth centuries most products were transported by road. The Industrial Revolution changed transportation needs as commodities had to be moved in far larger amounts than a horse and cart on a non-surfaced road could manage. A boat on a river route could carry greater quantities but not all areas could be accessed by navigable rivers. Entrepreneurial companies created narrow canals to allow waterways to reach all areas of the country and charged a toll to those who wanted to use them. Locks were used to enable canals to navigate areas with a gradient.

The industrialisation of Birmingham made it an important destination and companies fought to build canals to supply it. Birmingham has more canals than Venice and for many years, canals owned by different companies ran parallel to each other and just a few feet apart. The companies all charged different tariffs and were in constant competition with each other until the waterways were nationalised.

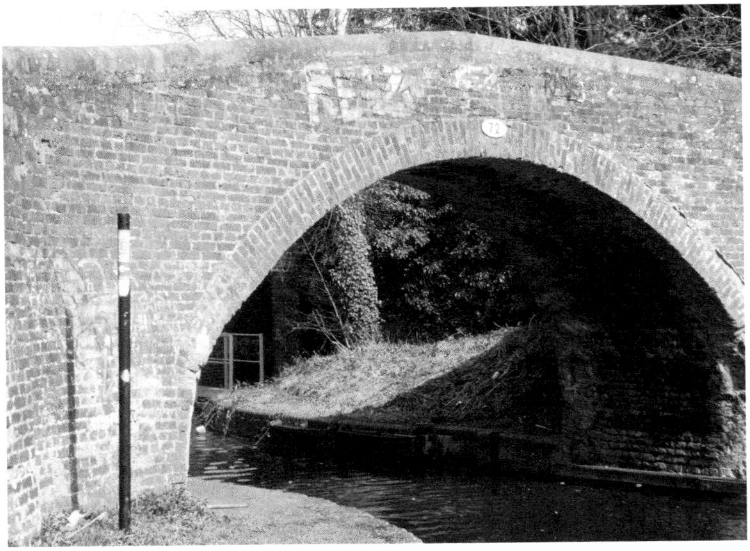

Birmingham's canals have moved from transportation purposes to leisure pursuits.

Horse-drawn narrowboats could carry a maximum of 30 tons and when the railways started to develop in the 1830s, it became apparent that they could transport far larger loads in less time. The canals gradually fell into decline. Birmingham city centre has 35 miles of waterways that are now used solely for recreation and leisure.

17. Birmingham Back to Backs (1831)

The last surviving back-to-back houses in Birmingham are on the corner of Inge and Hurst Streets. The Grade II listed properties are now owned by the National Trust, where they serve as a reminder of the housing conditions faced by urban workers during the Industrial Revolution.

At the turn of the nineteenth century, the Industrial Revolution caused the population of Birmingham to increase tenfold in just a few years. The owners of factories and mills rented out accommodation to their growing workforce and aimed to get the maximum number of people into the minimum amount of space. They constructed cheaply built tenements around a central courtyard, with one communal outhouse and a single standpipe. A family of eight or ten people would rent just one room and therefore hundreds of people lived in very close proximity. Typhus and cholera outbreaks were common occurrences and infant mortality reached a peak when 80 per cent of children did not reach their fifth birthday.

It was many years before reports about the shoddily built properties with unsanitary conditions began to reach parliament but finally, in 1875, the Public Health Act was passed. This ensured that any new housing had to follow strict guidelines but, as existing properties were exempt, the back-to-backs remained

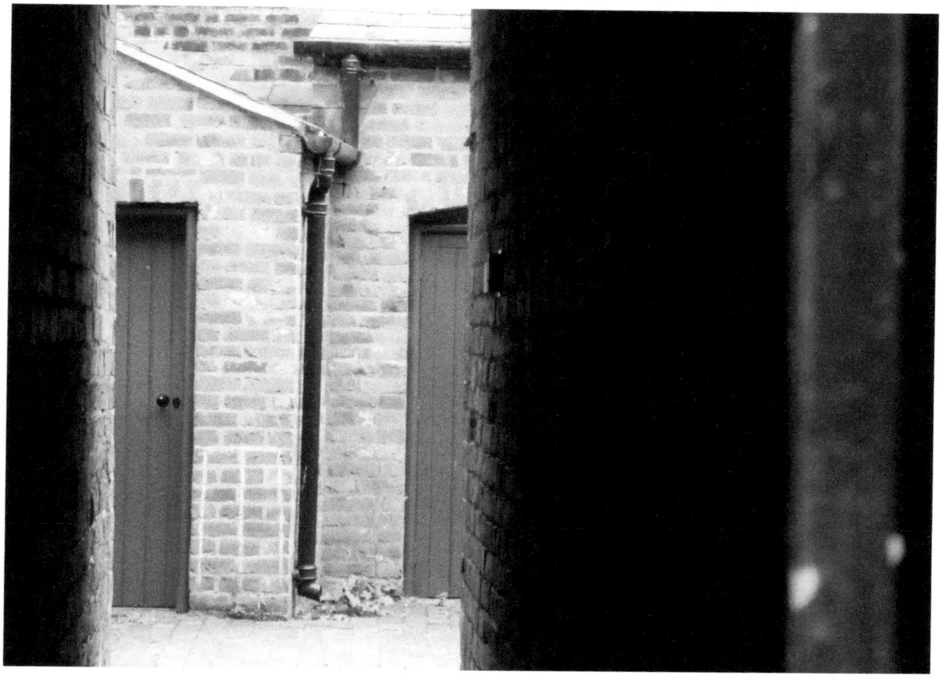

Birmingham back-to-backs were dark and cramped slums.

occupied. As they began to deteriorate to the point of dereliction, the owners of the back-to-backs reduced the rent and the occupants became only the poorest and roughest members of society. The back-to-backs became the slums of the city and synonymous with crime and disease.

Slum clearance began in the 1930s when better social housing became a government priority but Birmingham Back to Backs survived demolition because they were close to the affluent Jewellery Quarter. Most of the occupants had been home-working artisans in the area who kept the houses in relatively good condition. Some had been converted into workshops or jewellery retailers and, although Birmingham City Council declared the court unsuitable for domestic habitation in 1966, the businesses were allowed to remain.

In 1988 the back-to-backs were awarded a Grade II listing from Historic England due to their importance in the social history of Birmingham. The Birmingham Conservation Trust took on the task of completely restoring the site and it opened as a museum in 2004.

The restored Birmingham Back to Backs consist of houses and workshops clustered around a central courtyard accessed by a narrow alley. Multiple houses share one chimney stack with a communal fire grate and a restricted staircase leads to the three storeys of rooms. The realistic restoration gives insight into the cramped, claustrophobic and insanitary conditions of life during the Industrial Revolution.

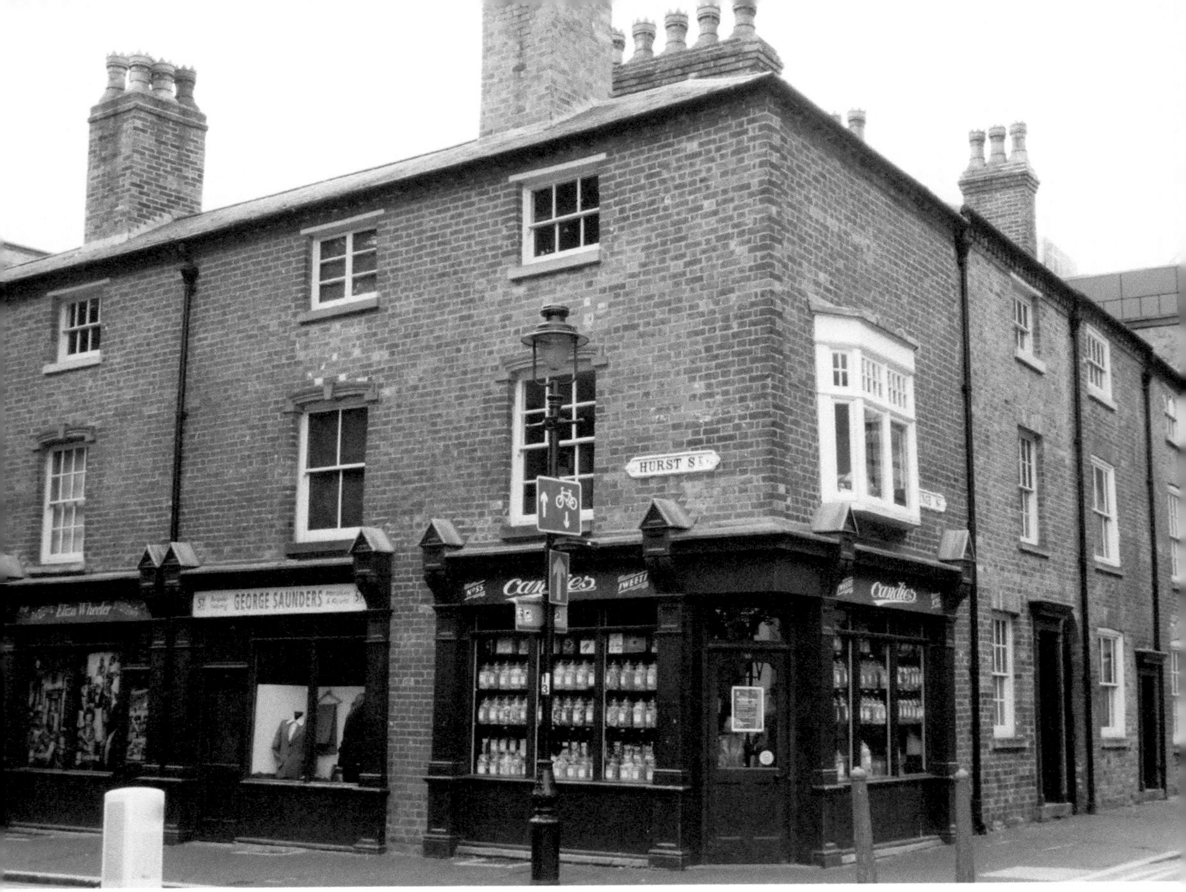

The corner site is now owned by The National Trust.

18. Town Hall (1834)

The Town Hall on Victoria Square is an imposing piece of classical architecture and a Grade I listed example of the Roman Revival style.

In 1834 a new music venue that was large enough to accommodate the burgeoning audiences of Birmingham was needed and a competition was held to design an appropriate concert building. Architects Edward Welch and Joseph Hansom submitted the winning plan for what was to become the first monumentally styled civic building in the country. It is called the Town Hall because public debates and government meetings were also held inside until the Council House was built in 1879.

The appearance of the building is based on the Temple of Castor and Pollux in ancient Rome. The podium is of rusticated stone from which the main body of the Town Hall rises on Corinthian pillars. The capital of each pillar has an elaborate floral decoration and form an impressive colonnade. The brick shell of the upper part of the building is faced with Welsh marble and the clean symmetry shown on all four sides of the exterior is preserved by placing the main entrance low in the podium.

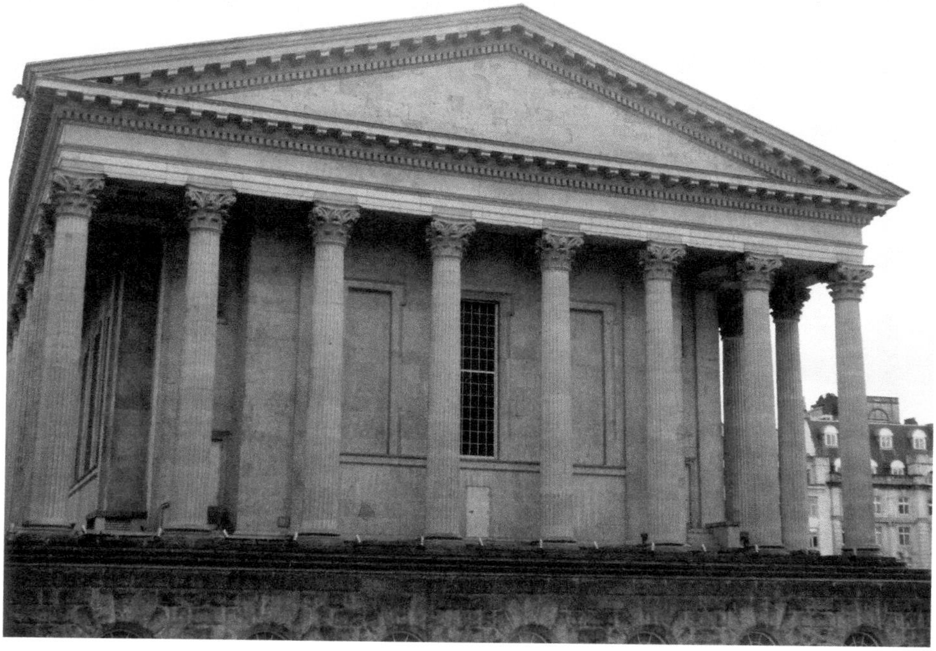

The Town Hall has a colonnade of Corinthian pillars.

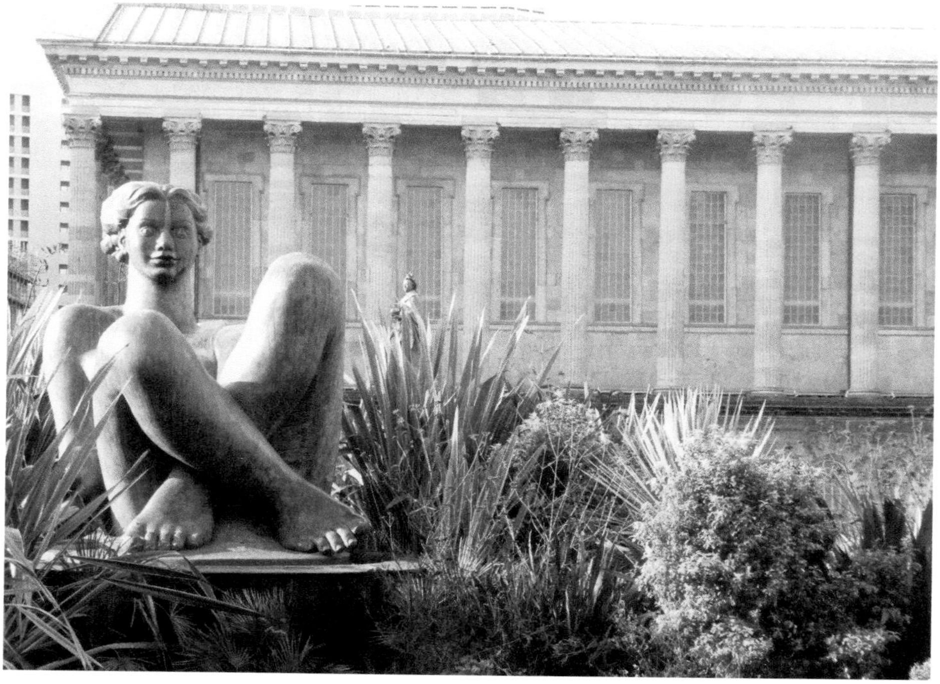

Victoria Square contains an interesting mix of statuary and architecture.

The interior of the building has been restored to its Georgian appearance. The architraves and ceiling of the auditorium have particularly detailed white plasterwork and the walls have been returned to their original blue colour scheme. The magnificent 1834 pipe organ dominates one wall and it was the first in Great Britain to have the pipes enclosed behind decorative screening. Birmingham City Council still employs a city organist to play this spectacular instrument at civic events.

The Town Hall has now been an exclusive concert venue for nearly two centuries. In its history it has premiered works by Gilbert and Sullivan, Mendelssohn and Elgar and Charles Dickens gave an atmospheric reading of his classic tale *A Christmas Carol* here in 1853.

19. Curzon Street Railway Station and Principal Building (1838)

In 1838, just a decade after railway pioneer George Stephenson produced the first steam locomotive, the London and Birmingham Railway company opened the first intercity main line, beginning the railway boom. Passengers could now travel between the two cities in around five hours and in comfortable surroundings not previously found in the carriage trip by road.

Curzon Street Principal Building has been listed Grade I.

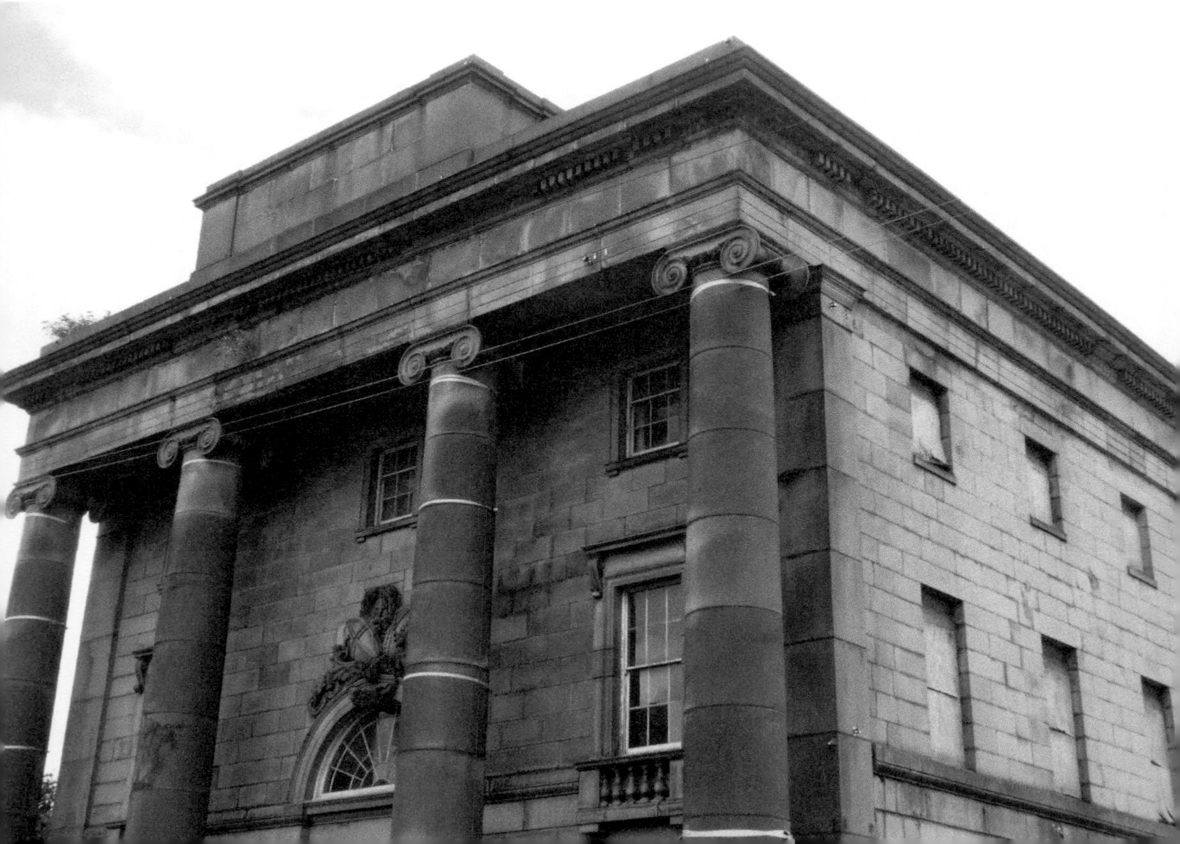

There was a main station at either end of the line designed by railway architect Philip Hardwick. He created Euston Station in London with a magnificent arch and Birmingham's Curzon Street Station. The Principal Building was the ticket office and refreshment area and it is the only part of Curzon Street that remains.

Hardwick's design only served Birmingham for twenty years however, as its location was considered inconvenient and the more centrally placed New Street Station was built instead. Curzon Street continued to be used for local travel until 1893 but after that it was only used for goods. The Principal Building was awarded a Grade I listing in 1952 and fortunately could not be demolished when Curzon Street Station was dismantled in the 1960s. The ground around it has since been cleared for development of the high-speed rail link between Birmingham and London. The proposal is to return it to its original purpose of entrance hall and ticket office.

The Curzon Street Principal Building is the oldest surviving piece of monumental railway architecture in the world and its exterior is largely unaltered. It is built in Greek Revival style with unadorned Ionic columns and is typical of late Palladian design. The square building has three storeys with a flat lead and slate roof. The central doorway has a decorative fan light surmounted by a carved tablet bearing the London and Birmingham Railway Company coat of arms.

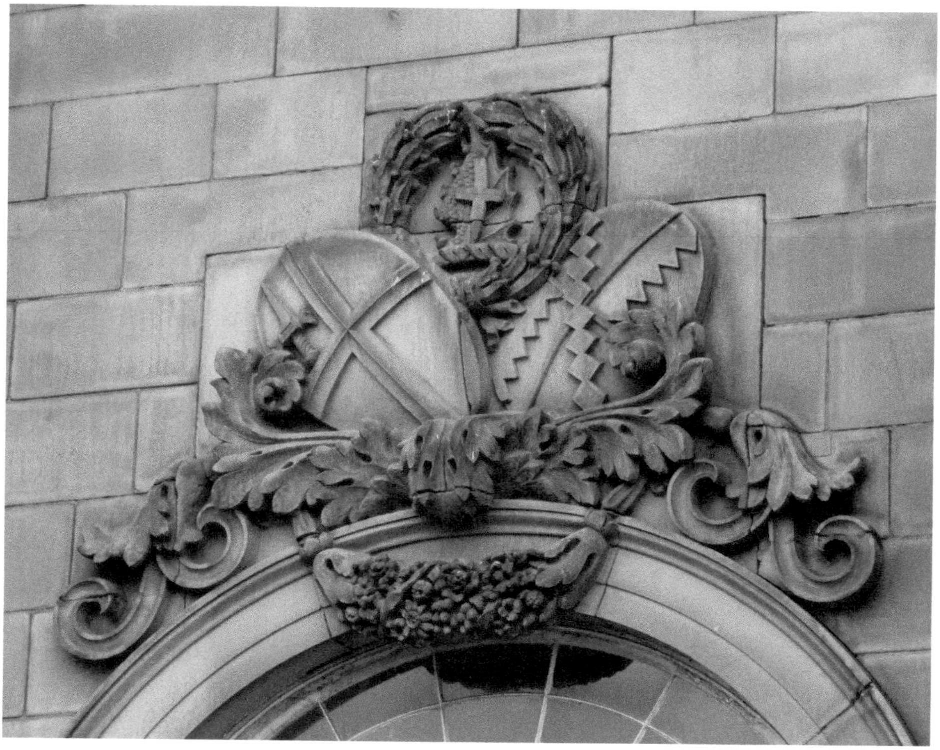

The London and Birmingham Railway was completed in 1838.

20. St Chad's Cathedral (1841)

St Chad's Roman Catholic Cathedral was surrounded by the Gun Quarter and its community when it was built in 1841. The area changed dramatically after the redevelopment of Birmingham in the 1960s and the cathedral now stands on Queensway, the main duel carriageway through the city.

St Chad's was the first Catholic cathedral commissioned after an Act of Parliament finally repealed the sixteenth century outlawing of Catholicism by Henry VIII. After being unable to practise their faith for so long, the Catholic Church lacked funds and therefore their new cathedral needed to be as inexpensive as possible. The only site they could afford to buy was a narrow, sloped plot in Birmingham and skilled architect Augustus Welby Northmore Pugin was appointed to create a suitable plan. His design was in a Gothic style and the influence of fourteenth-century German churches can be seen in the needle spires on the west tower. Pugin used red brick throughout, which was both inexpensive and quicker to work with than stone, thereby cutting labour costs.

St Chad's Cathedral is one of architect Pugin's finest works.

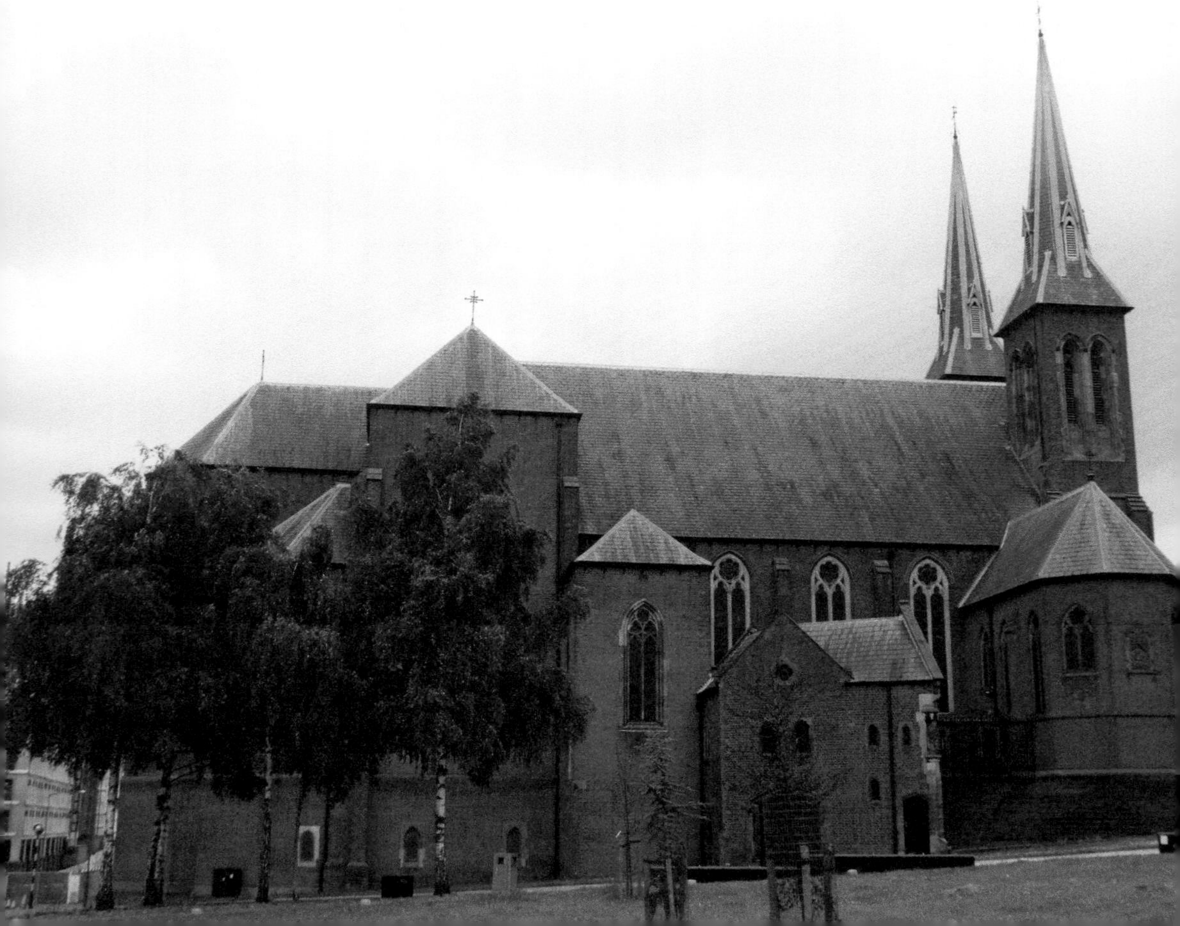

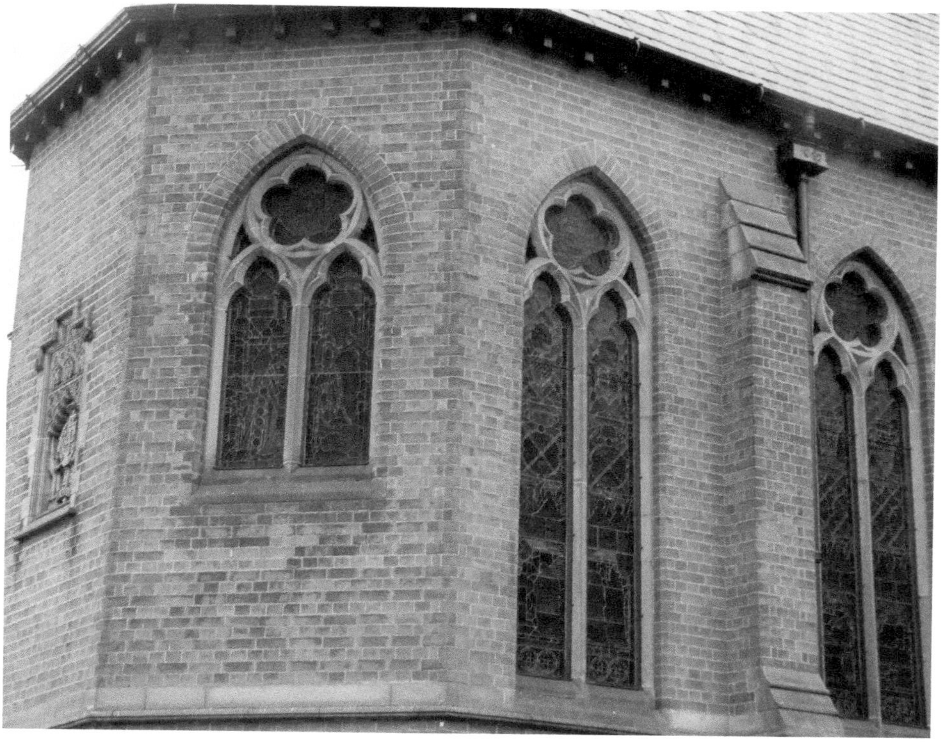

Red brick has been used to create the Gothic style.

St Chad's has a Grade II listing due to its historical importance. Above the altar is a reliquary containing the bones of St Chad, a seventh-century martyr. The relics had been kept in Lichfield cathedral until the Dissolution of the Monasteries, when they were saved from destruction by a priest who passed them to a loyal catholic family. The casket containing St Chad's bones remained safely hidden for generations. When the new Pugin cathedral needed an appropriate saint to be dedicated to, the relics were passed back into the hands of the Catholic Church and consequently the cathedral was dedicated to St Chad.

The altar is under a wooden canopy designed by Pugin, as is the bishop's chair and choir screen. The pulpit and canons stalls contain fifteenth-century timber from medieval originals brought from Germany. Pugin also designed the stained-glass windows in the Gothic style and he based the ceiling paintings on medieval originals found in Ely cathedral. The nave is lined with narrow wooden pillars decorated in gold leaf and Pugin originally added many more embellishments to the interior. However, in 1965, the Second Vatican Council wanted to modernise the Catholic Church and ordered the removal and overpainting of ornamentation in churches and cathedrals. Many of Pugin's designs were removed, although his large representation of Christ crucified was later restored.

21. Singer's Hill Synagogue (1856)

Most medieval towns had a Jewish community but none was recorded in Birmingham until the eighteenth century after the vast increase in population during the Industrial Revolution brought diverse communities into the town. A small building was converted from a private dwelling for worship but soon an official synagogue was needed. Yeoville Thomason, the award-winning architect who later designed Birmingham's Council House, was commissioned for the design and the new synagogue was finished in 1856. Despite the building's modest size, the synagogue has become known as Birmingham's cathedral synagogue due to the grandeur of its design.

Singer's Hill Synagogue has a classical red-brick construction and the tri-part façade of the building has exceptional symmetry. The Romanesque design has detailing completed in yellow and grey bricks. An Italianate three-arch arcade with canopy forms the entrance and is central to the property. Above this is a magnificent wheel window with etched glass and stone traceries. The side wings have round headed windows with stone surrounds and leaded door canopies project forwards to great architectural effect.

The interior is furnished with excellent examples of nineteenth-century woodwork including the gallery. It has a barrel-vaulted ceiling that is painted with a classical colour scheme of pale blue with white and gold decoration and is hung with chandeliers. The twentieth-century stained glass in the side windows adds further colour.

Birmingham's synagogue dates from 1856.

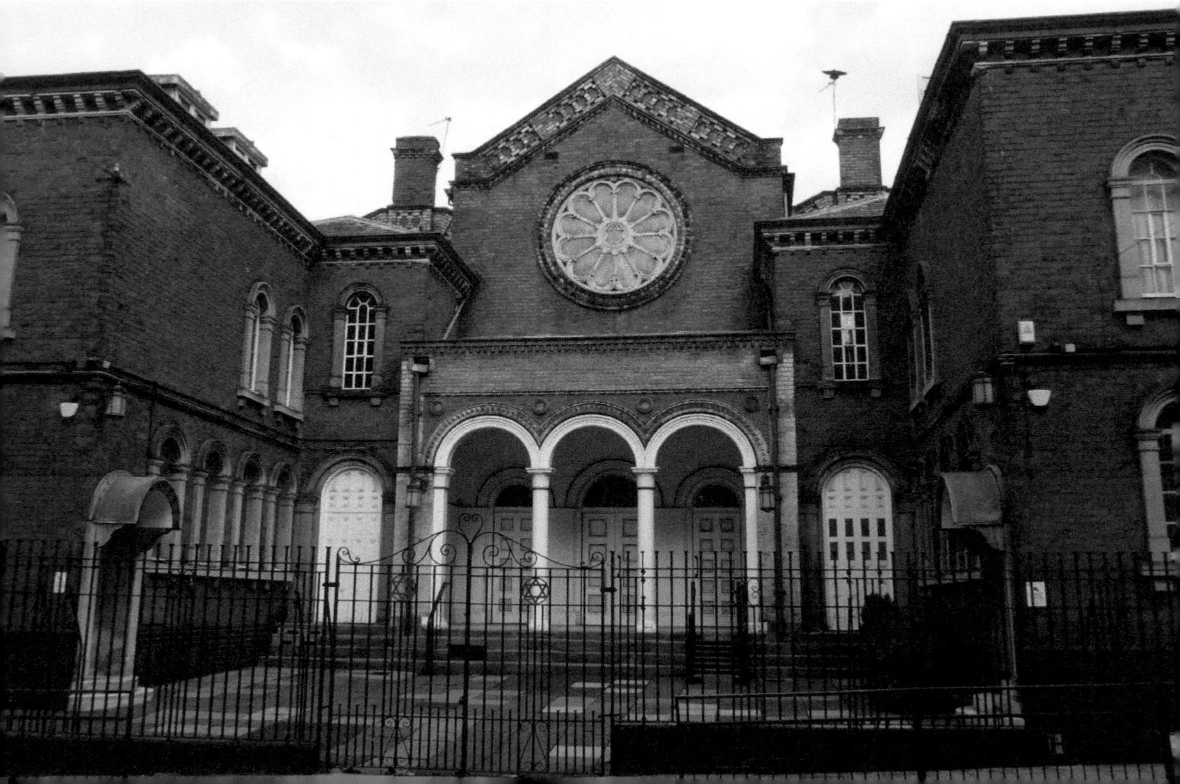

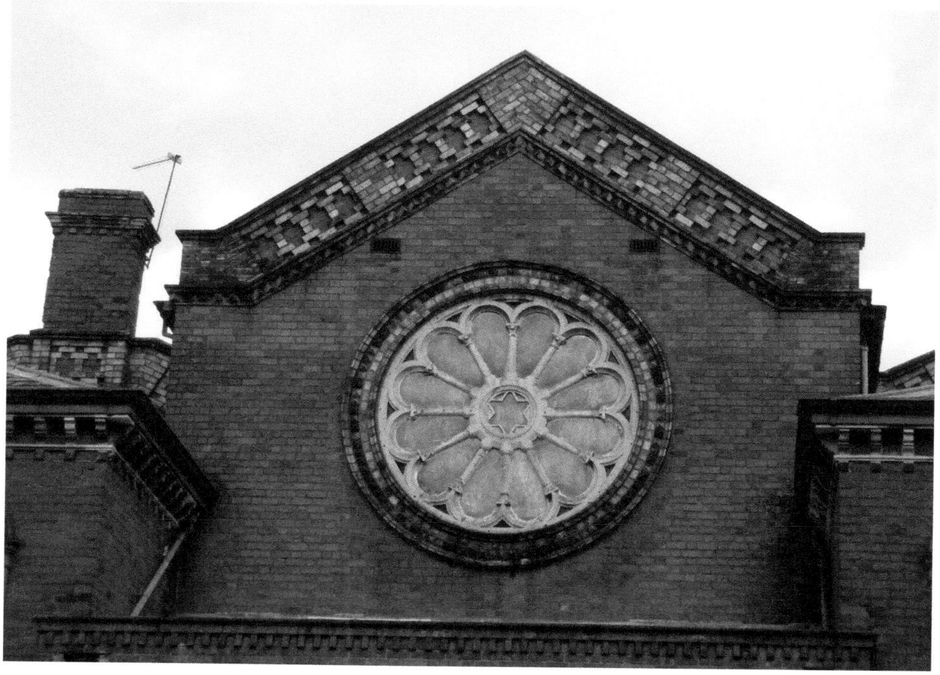

A traceried wheel window and brick detailing add decoration.

22. St Martin in the Bullring (1873)

There has been a church dedicated to St Martin on the same spot in the Bullring for nearly a thousand years, although it has been rebuilt. The Grade II listed church that now occupies the site was built in 1873.

The name Bullring is derived from the medieval practice of bull-baiting. It is not the arena where spectators would gather that it is named after, but the permanent ring in the ground to which the bull was tethered. It was also the marketplace and, as the heart of the town, the site of the first St Martin's Church in the twelfth century.

The market grew, shops were built on nearby streets and the area prospered. However, deterioration of the medieval church created a need to rebuild it and in 1873, local architect J. A. Chatwin was commissioned. The Gothic design was similar to the original with stone-built walls and a tall, timber beamed nave. The floor tiles were all made by Staffordshire potters Minton and the stained-glass windows included one made by William Morris to a Burne-Jones design. Medieval wall paintings were saved when the original church was rebuilt and can be seen inside.

Birmingham was remodelled during the mid-twentieth century and St Martin's was renovated. However, the shops and markets of the old Bullring were demolished. The replacement Bullring Shopping Centre was an icon in 1960s design and Great Britain's first shopping mall.

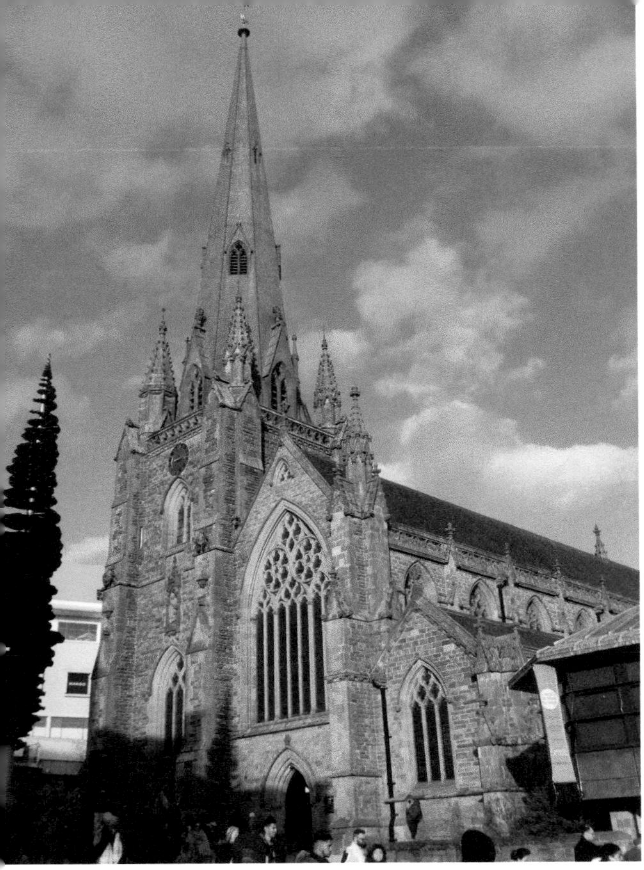

Left: St Martin in the Bullring has Victorian Gothic style.

Below: The Bullring has been a trading place for a millennium.

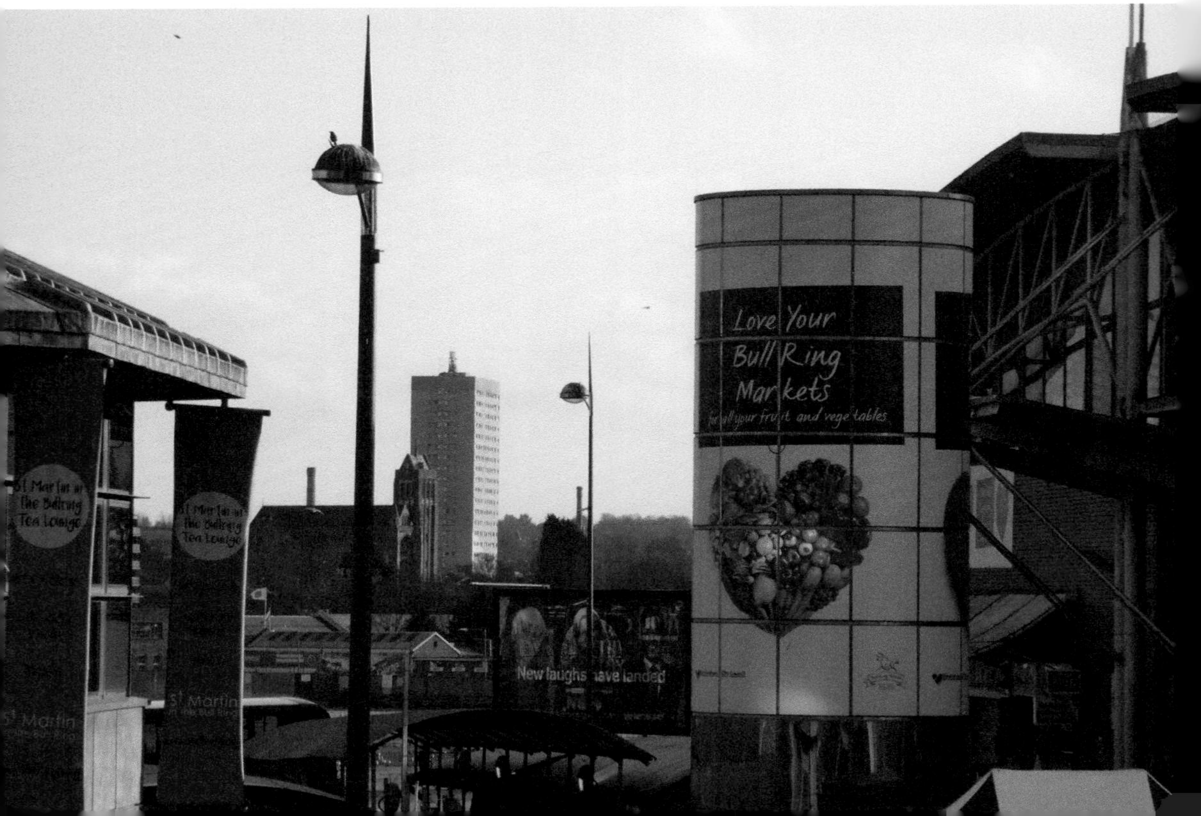

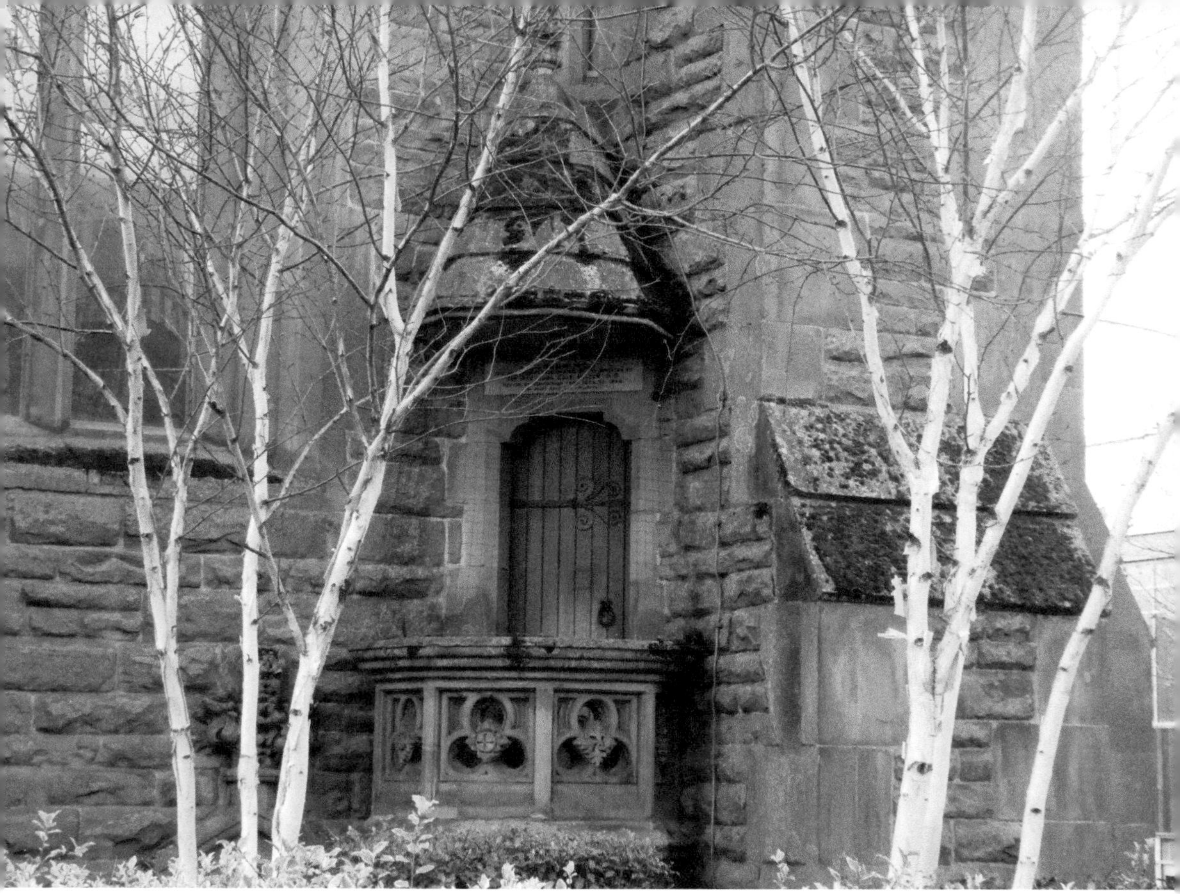

A unique outdoor pulpit is for preaching to shoppers.

It was built in concrete using the brutalist style and was considered 'space age' due to air conditioning and piped music. However, it was not popular with visitors as the mall was surrounded by dual carriageways and accessed via subways and escalators that rarely worked. The Bullring was designed as the essence of modernity but became an example of the 'concrete jungle' that 1960s Birmingham was known as. The Bullring was updated at the turn of the twenty-first century.

St. Martin's still stands in the centre of the shopping area. The church has a rare outdoor pulpit and it has regularly been used to preach to shoppers as they pass by.

23. Great Western Arcade (1876)

The Great Western Arcade was built in 1876. The prestigious precinct of high-quality shops was symbolic of Victorian Birmingham's affluence. The covered passageway linked wealthy Colmore Row with Temple Row and also disguised the cutting made for the Great Western Railway. The arrival of the railway brought people into central Birmingham but the engineering was unattractive. Constructing a shopping arcade over the railway made the area more attractive to the eye and also attracted potential consumers.

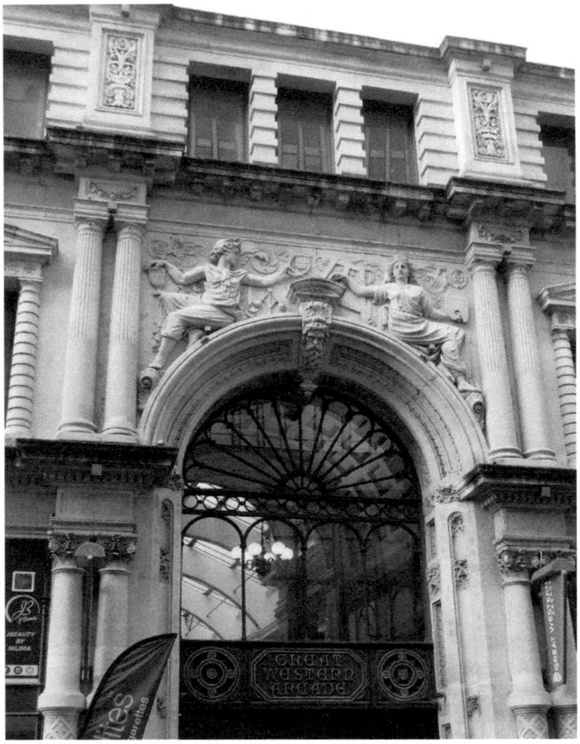

Left: The Great Western Arcade appealed to wealthy Victorian consumers.

Below: Interior features of the mall remain unchanged.

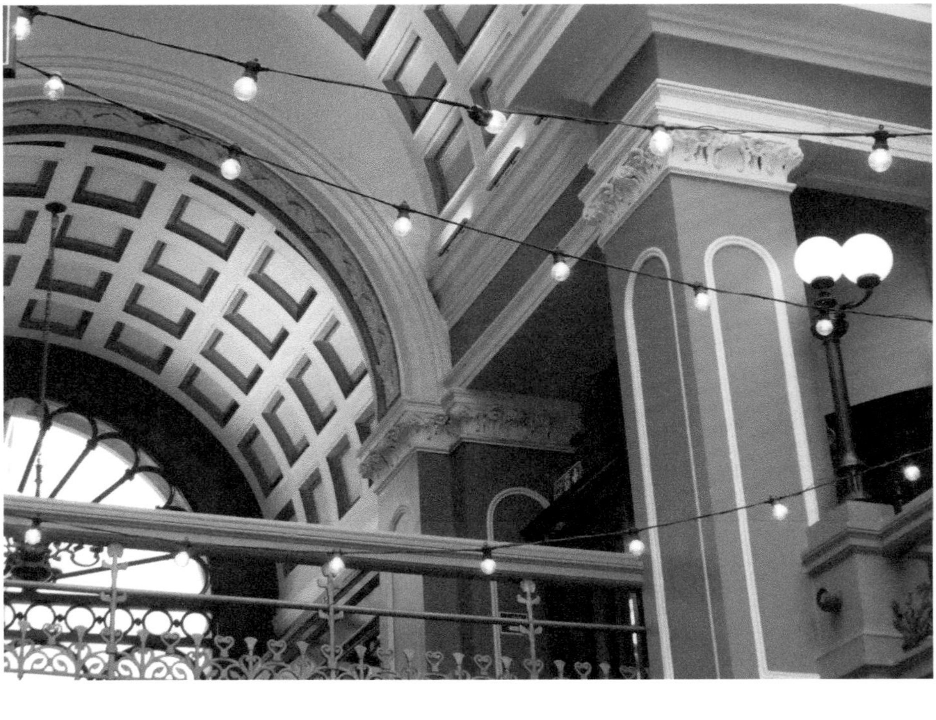

The commission for the design went to local architect W. H. Ward. Ward was a great admirer of Joseph Paxton, the designer of the Crystal Palace in London, and this influence was evident in the arcade's fully glazed barrel-vaulted roof. The original roof had a central dome but it was lost in a fire in the Second World War. The replacement was to a simpler design but retained the light and airy atmosphere.

The pedestrian access at Colmore Row suffered bomb damage at the same time and was later rebuilt with a modern frontage but the Temple Row entrance has retained its monumental splendour. The vast stone portal is flanked with Corinthian-style pilasters and there is a large and ornate classical entablature to welcome shoppers. The original semicircular windows below the frieze are iconic of the Great Western Arcade and are now used in its logo.

The interior of the mall has patterned tiled floors and the shopfronts are all original. The mezzanine gallery is as it was in the nineteenth century, although the chandeliers and gaslights have been replaced. The independent, artisan retail units in the Great Western Arcade have preserved the fashionable decadence of its Victorian heritage.

24. Assay Office (1878/2015)

Birmingham's Assay Office, as one of the largest hallmarking sites in the world, had to relocate to Icknield Street in 2015 when the original office on Newhall Street no longer had the capacity to process the twelve million items of precious metal that need evaluating each year.

There is a long history of metal-craft in the city. Hallmarking precious metals has been a legal requirement since the fourteenth century, when gold and silver smiths were legally required to go to London for assessment of their products. Birmingham's renown for manufacturing fine metalwork burgeoned in the eighteenth century and the logistics involved with having to take each piece to London for assaying was a problem. Matthew Boulton wanted to promote the craftsmanship of Birmingham and used his status as successful industrialist to get parliamentary permission for a local assay office. This was granted in 1773.

The first assay office was just a rented room but by 1878, a large purpose-built site was proposed and the architect Andrew Phipson was commissioned to design the office on Newhall Street. The red brick building has a restrained Italianate design with a centrally sited, stone-faced porch and polished granite detailing leading the eye up to the first floor. Here a pilastered arch is topped with a coat of arms entablature.

The property was awarded a Grade II listing for specialist historical interest in 2004, as it was still being used for its original purpose. In 2015, however, the Assay Office had to move out to larger premises.

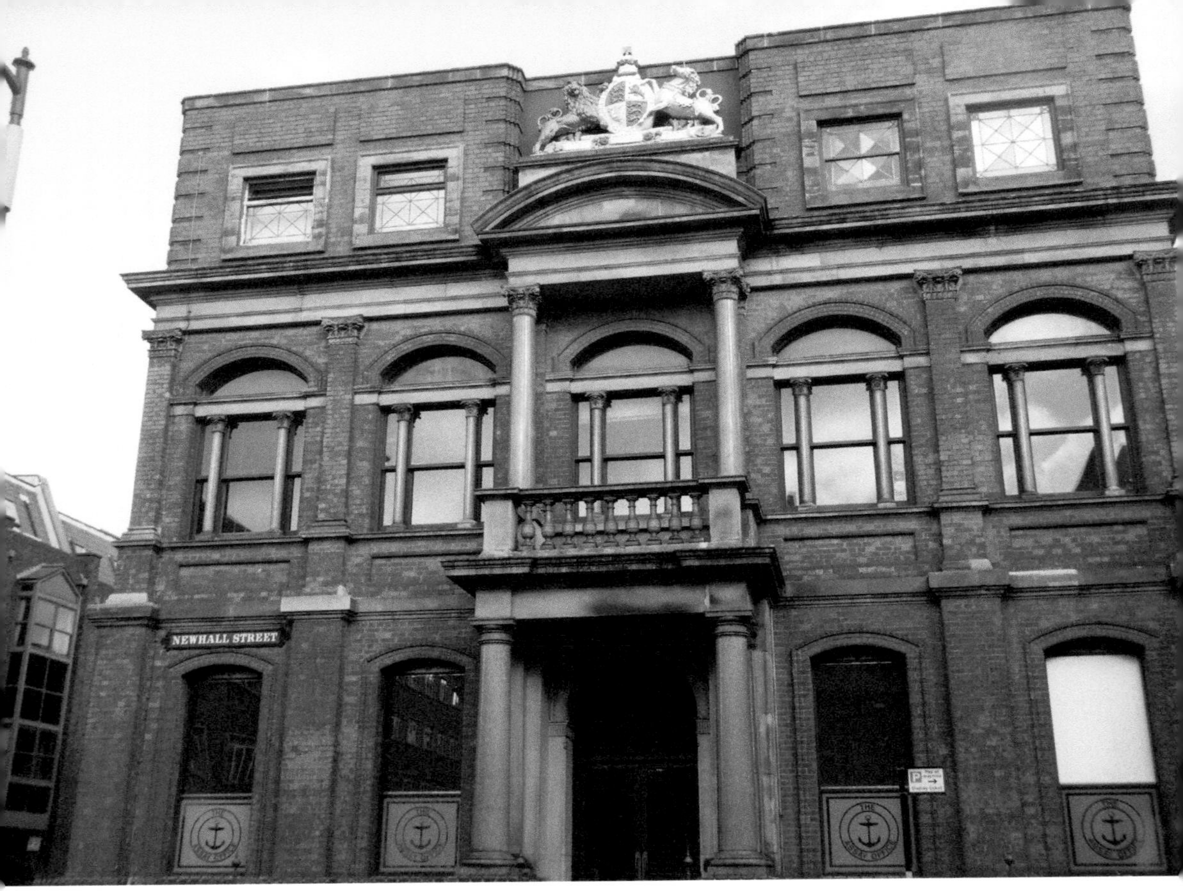

Birmingham's Assay Office was important to local commerce.

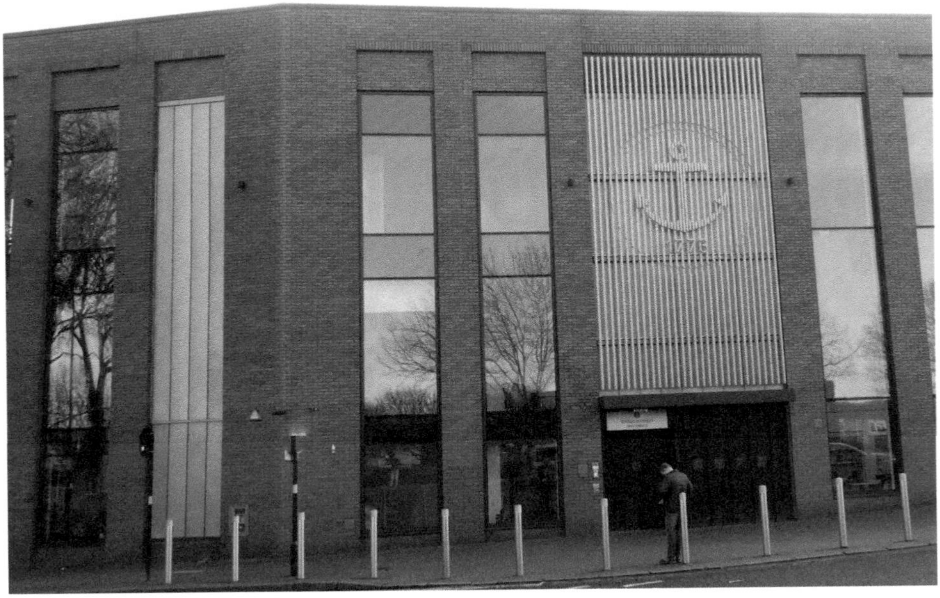

The new Assay Office hallmarks 12 million items per year.

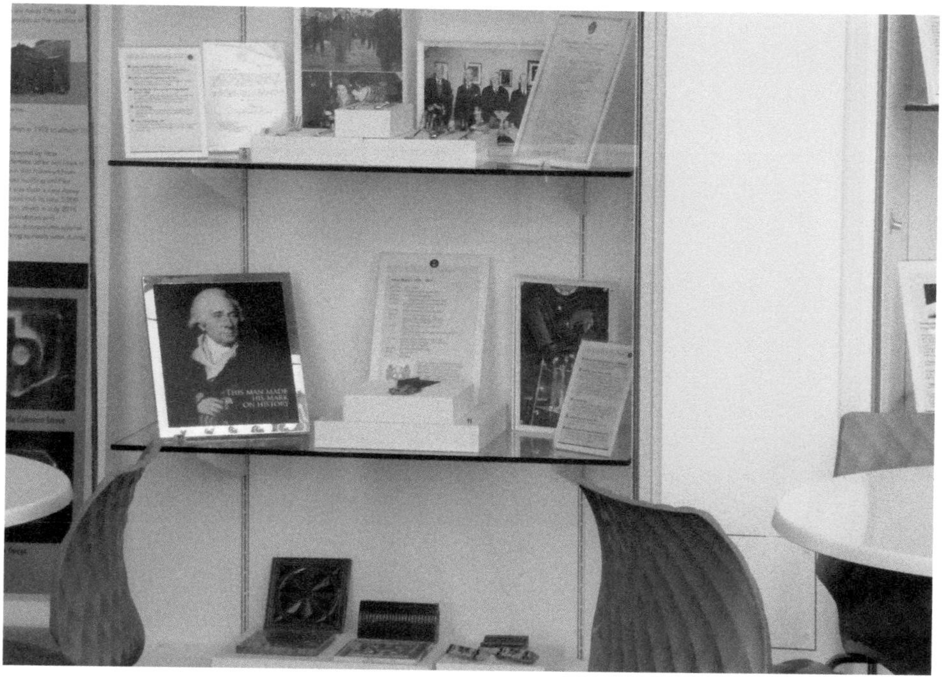

Local precious metalwork is displayed in a small museum.

The new property on Icknield Street was built in 2015 as part of a major scheme to revamp the conservation area around the Jewellery Quarter. The blue brick industrial style building blends into a landscape which consists mostly of Georgian and Victorian factories. The construction uses blue rather than red brick to stand out from its historical counterparts. It has been designed as a two-storey property with vertical strip glazing to let in the maximum amount of light and cut energy costs. In addition to being responsible for checking the purity of metals and gems, the building also houses a library containing important texts relating to assaying and a small museum of historically important local metalwork.

25. Highbury Hall (1878)

Highbury Hall is surrounded by tranquil gardens and a 100-acre parkland estate. It was built in 1878 for Birmingham's mayor and Member of Parliament Joseph Chamberlain, who wanted it to be his *rus en urbe*. The expression translates to 'countryside in the city' and was a term used by wealthy Victorians to denote the grand estates they created in urban settings.

Highbury Hall is on Yew Tree Road in the Mosely area of Birmingham and was designed by Birmingham architect J. H. Chamberlain in a Venetian Gothic style. The red-brick house has naturalistic detailing in terracotta, stone and timber.

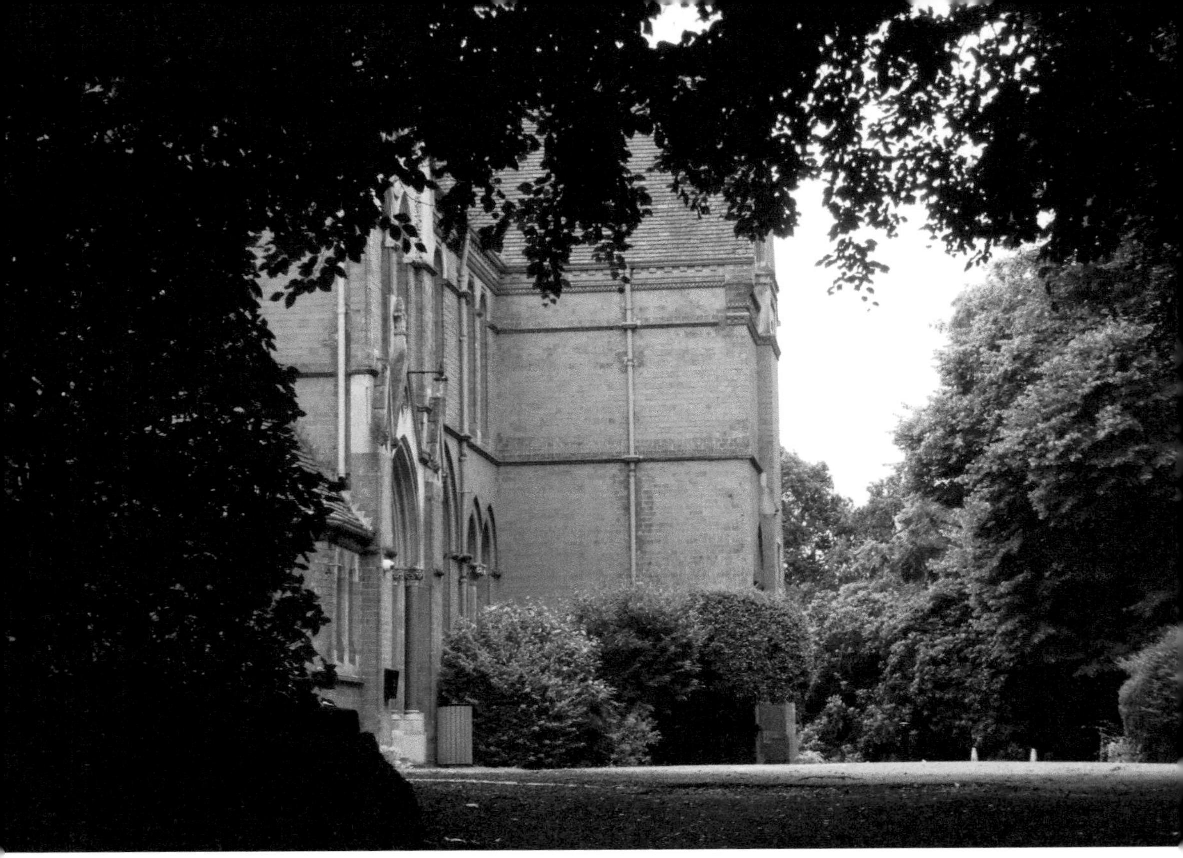

Wealthy Victorians created inner-city country estates.

The intricately carved brickwork on the gable ends reveals influence from the Arts and Crafts movement and bold bays to the front of the building give it visual impact.

Historic England has awarded Highbury Hall a Grade II listing as both the exterior and the interior have retained their original features. The great hall has a fine wooden floor, the patina of which is also found in the panelled walls and doors. A pink marble fireplace surmounted by a triptych-style mirror is at one end of this large room and the other end is dominated by the staircase, which rises behind a series of archways to a gallery with intricate wrought-iron railings. Pink marble pilasters and timber panelling can be found throughout the house and these create an atmosphere of continuity.

During his lifetime, Joseph Chamberlain was a notable and respected mayor for Birmingham and was responsible for implementing many upgrades to living conditions in the city. He used Highbury Hall as the venue for parliamentary dinner parties where he persuaded his political colleagues to agree with his social improvement policies and pass them through Westminster.

Highbury Hall is now used as a venue for conferences and weddings. It was sold to Birmingham City Council by the Chamberlain family and was initially used as an auxiliary hospital for wounded servicemen during the First World War. It has since passed to a private hospitality company and has been completely restored.

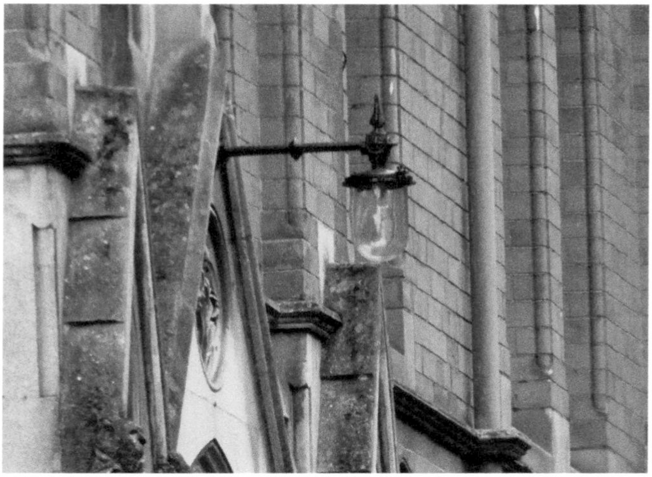

Decorative features on Highbury Hall are Arts and Crafts style.

26. Cadbury Chocolate Factory (1879)

The Cadbury Chocolate Factory was designed by architect George Gadd and opened in 1879. Surrounded by the model village of Bournville, it was called the factory in a garden due to its setting in the then rural area just 4 miles out of the centre of Birmingham.

Chocolate manufacturing takes place in the lovely setting of Bournville.

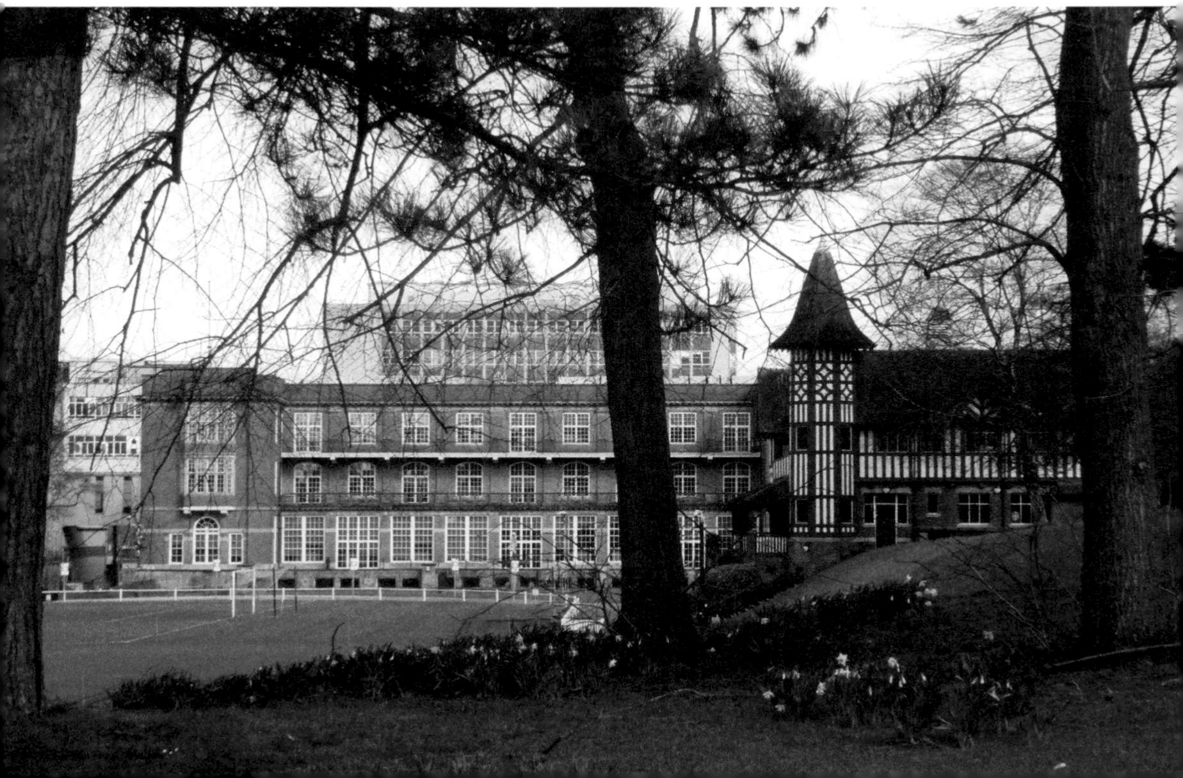

The site was chosen by George Cadbury when the company needed to expand out of the city centre. Cadbury was a philanthropist and used a lot of the company profits for the welfare of his workers. He wanted an area large enough to create housing and move his workforce out of the cramped city slums.

George Cadbury also supported many charitable organisations and when the First World War began, he donated boxes of chocolates, books and clothing for those fighting overseas. He also gave over two company buildings for conversion into hospitals for wounded soldiers. Inspired by their employer's kindness and generosity many factory staff volunteered in the hospital in their spare time.

The Cadbury story began in 1824 when John Cadbury started a business selling loose tea, coffee and drinking chocolate in the centre of Birmingham. He began to manufacture his own chocolate powder and opened a factory on Bridge Street in 1831. The business passed to sons Richard and George and after Richard died in 1899, George went on to launch Cadbury Dairy Milk, which has led the confectionery market since 1905.

In 1879 the factory was surrounded by open space, lawns and gardens. Even today a lot of the Cadbury site consists of grassed areas and playing fields. The original block of the factory complex is a straightforward industrial design built with a stone ground floor and red-brick upper storeys. There are columns of windows to let in the maximum amount of natural light, but all were designed to open wide to stop the employees from getting too hot in the summer. The names Cadbury and Bournville are spelled out in cream faience tiles on two faces of the factory building to add decoration to the plain design. Although the factory has been expanded over the years, all of the newer blocks have been designed with employee welfare and the environment in mind.

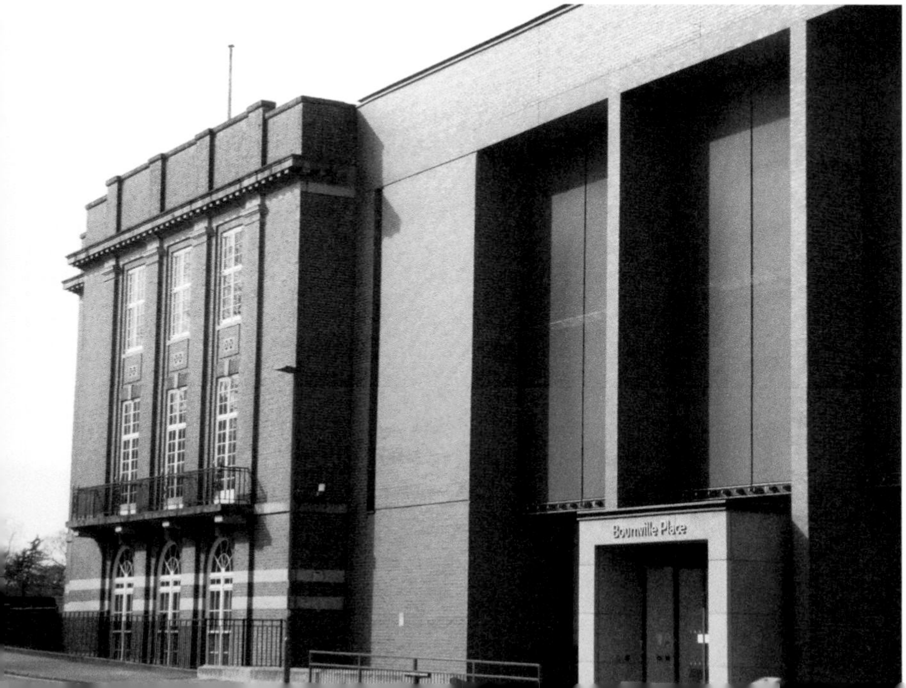

Cadbury factory buildings have a simple and attractive design.

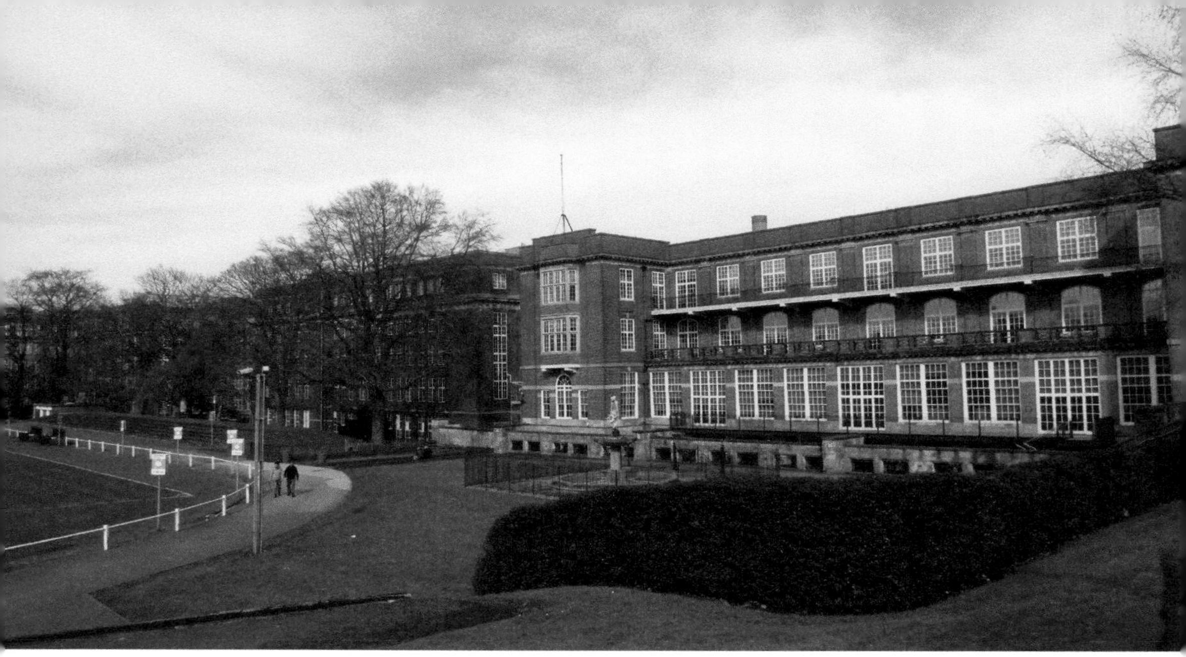

Dairy Milk has been made here for over a century.

The oldest part of the building was where Cadbury Dairy Milk was first produced in its iconic purple wrapper. This has become the family attraction Cadbury World, which celebrates all things chocolate.

27. Council House (1879)

The large Romanesque Council House is the focal point of Victoria Square. Although Gothic architecture was popular in the 1870s, the council wanted a monumental style and a classical design by Birmingham architect Yeoville Thomason was used.

The foundation stone of the building was laid by the Lord Mayor of Birmingham, Sir Joseph Chamberlain, in 1874 and he also hosted the grand opening in 1879. Sir Joseph Chamberlain was elected mayor three times and worked tirelessly in government. Some claim he has still not left the Council House. Over a century after his death there have reportedly been sightings of him standing behind the desk that he used when he was in office.

Six years after the Council House opened a block was added in which to house Birmingham Museum and Art Gallery. In 1919, interior access between the two separate buildings was achieved by constructing a first-floor walkway. The covered arch is in keeping with the Italianate style of the building and was designed to resemble the Bridge of Sighs in Venice.

The Council House has been given a Grade II listing by Historic England. Its large frontage is dominated by the central bay where the main entrance consists of a large portico of columns supporting a balcony. The front rail of the balcony is set with a series of stone lions and at the rear is a Murano glass mosaic depicting

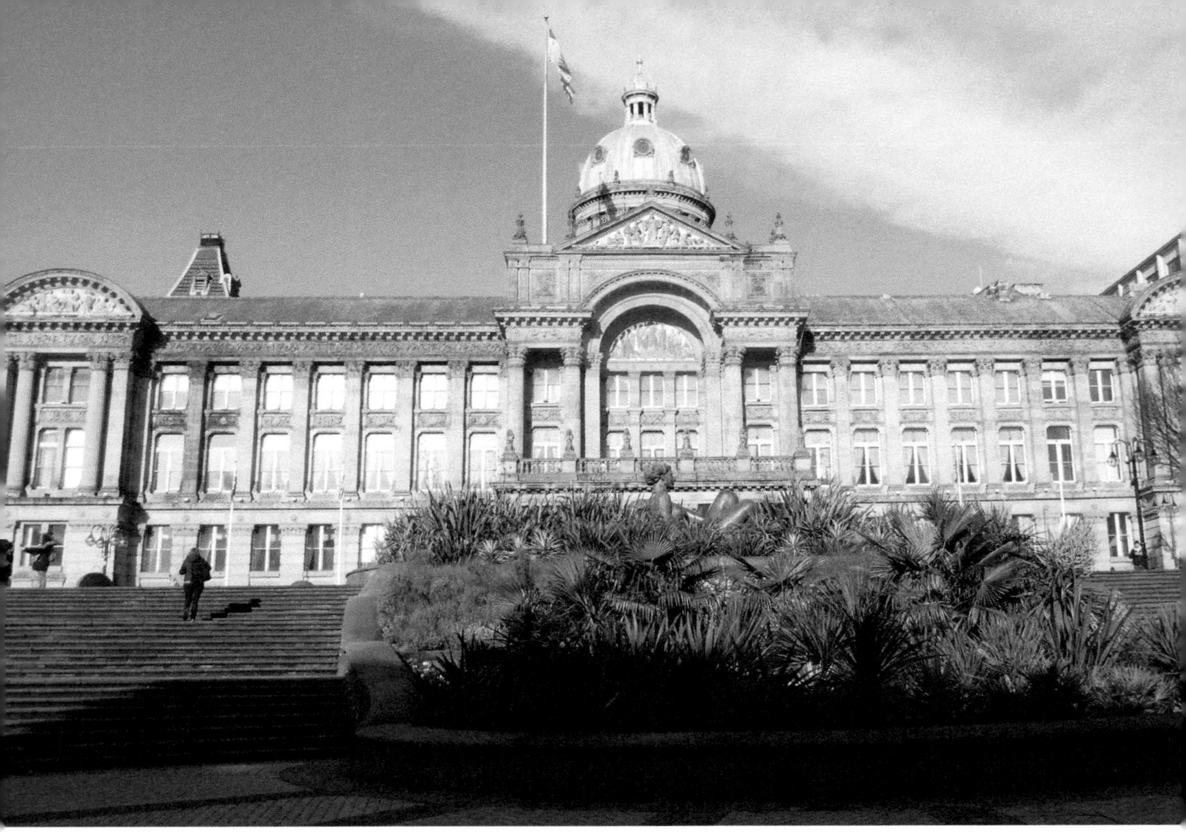

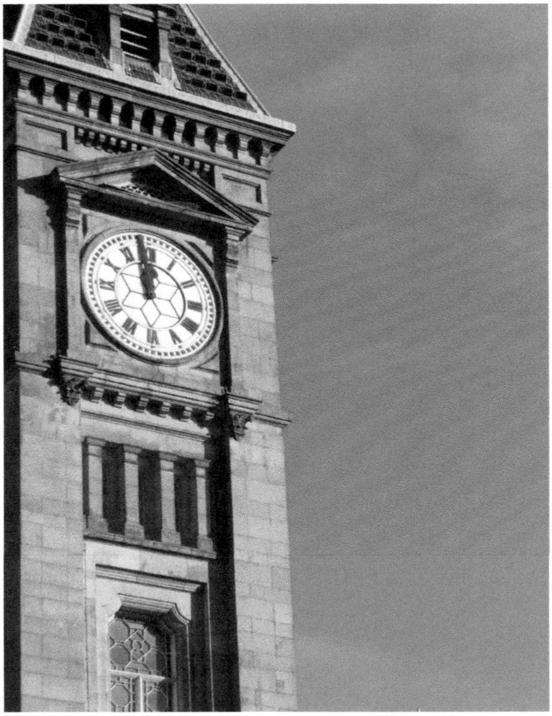

Above: The classically designed Council House is in a commanding position.

Left: Birmingham's skyline has a clock tower whimsically called Big Brum.

Britannia receiving the manufacturers of Birmingham. This image is repeated in the tympanum on the roofline. Arched pediments and a series of Corinthian pilasters decorate the stone exterior alongside moulded borders and friezes between the windows. The clock tower is the focal point of the roofline and known affectionately as Big Brum.

The interior has many original fittings including highly decorated pillars and pilasters. At the top of the marble staircase in the Museum and Art Gallery is a fresco by Joseph Southall, one of Birmingham's leading artists of the Arts and Crafts movement.

The steps of Victoria Square lead up to the main entrance of the Council House and incorporate a sculpture called *The River*. This was originally a water feature by sculptor Dhruva Mistry but it was prone to developing leaks and eventually could not be repaired. The water was removed and replaced by shrubs and flowers.

28. Grand Hotel (1879)

In 1879, property developer Isaac Horton built a commercial guest house on Colmore Row. Architect Thomson Plevins' design incorporated exhibition rooms where transient salesman could display their products, but it was not a great success.

In 1890, the interior was completely remodelled to become a luxury hotel. An extension was added with a hundred bedrooms and all had gas lighting and hot and cold running water. Public facilities included shops and hairdressers and the

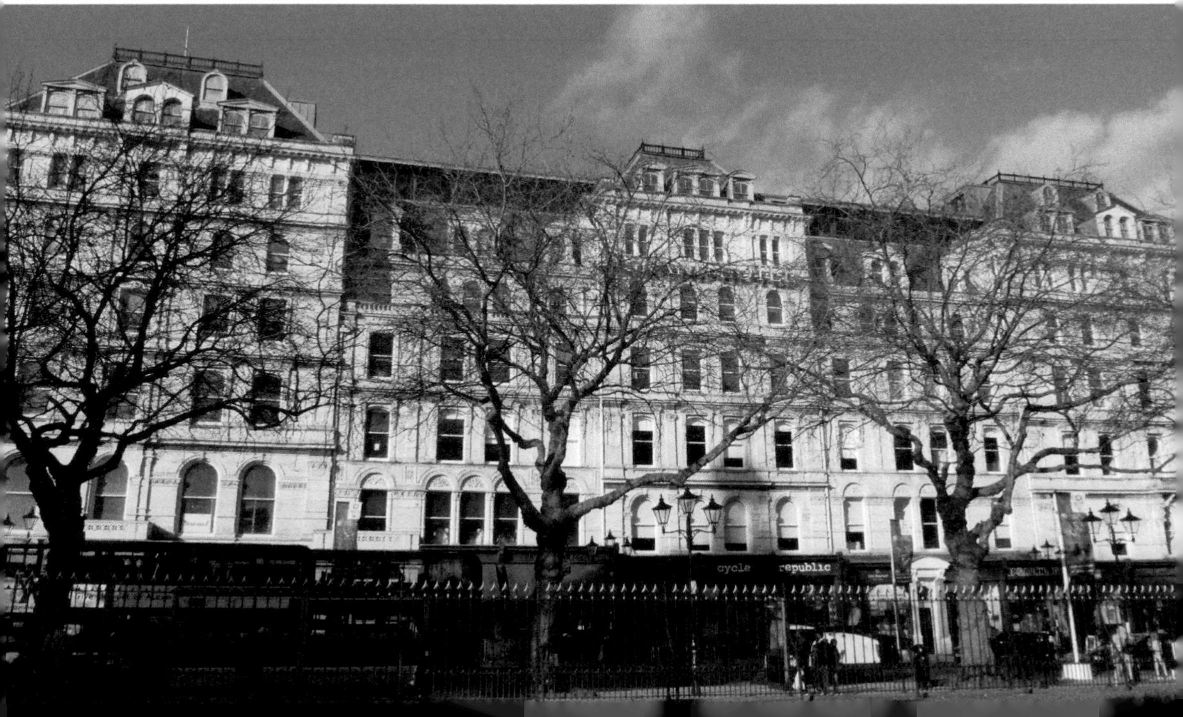

The Grand Hotel attracted only the wealthiest members of society.

hotel's Grosvenor Room became the finest venue in Birmingham for functions. For around fifty years the Grand was one of the most elite hotels in England.

The hotel changed hands many times during the twentieth century and its success gradually declined. Essential repairs to the fabric of the building were ignored and eventually the cost of repair became unviable and there were moves to demolish it.

Aware of the historical value of the building, the Victorian Society fought to save it. They issued an application to Historic England to get the hotel listed and this was granted in 2004. Despite the high expense of repairing and renovating a listed building, an eight-year restoration was begun in 2012 to turn the Grand back into a luxury hotel.

The design of the hotel reflects the palatial splendour of the French Renaissance with a whitewashed stone façade, decorative window surrounds and slate mansard roofs. It is visually divided into five distinct bays and has six storeys, including attic rooms with dormer windows. The height of the hotel balances its length and symmetry is created by the use of pilasters and rows of windows.

The interior of the hotel retains its oak doors, grand marble staircase and Victorian reception rooms. Of these the Grosvenor Room is still the most impressive. There are marble pilasters and minstrel's galleries where musicians played at balls and functions and the ceiling has highly ornate plasterwork which includes cherubs supporting scrolled pediments. Suspended from it are large art deco-style lights, which complement the surrounding Victoriana.

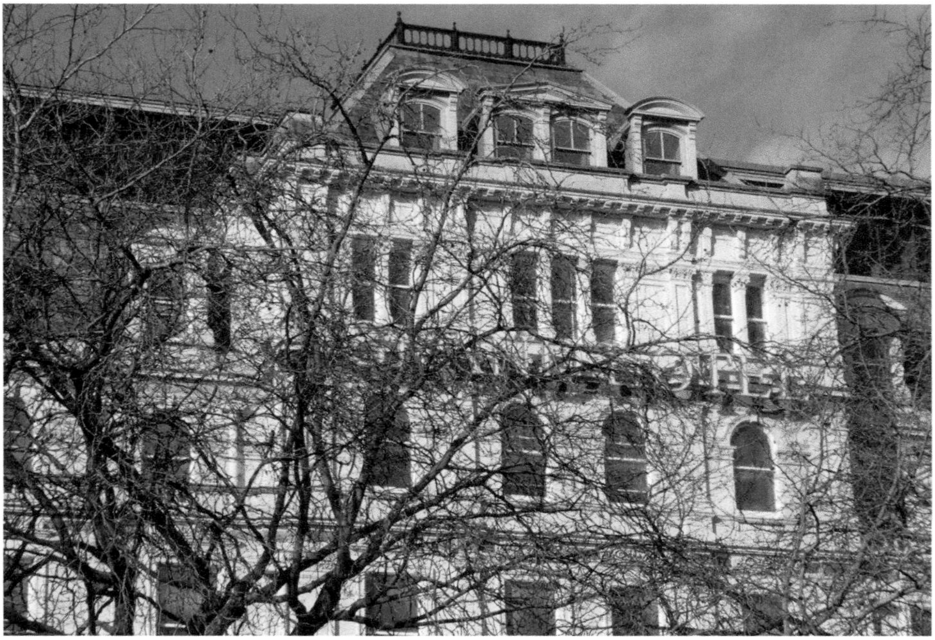

Mansard roofs and dormer windows reflect a French Renaissance influence.

29. Birmingham School of Art (1885)

Birmingham School of Art was the first specifically built public art school in Great Britain. The Victorian government wanted to improve the standard of British design and proposed a school to encourage artists. Birmingham architect J. H. Chamberlain was commissioned to design the school in 1885 and the Royal Birmingham Society of Artists began their teaching.

The Grade I listed building on Margaret Street is an impressive Victorian Gothic building and a testament to the ethos of the Arts and Crafts movement, who centred around the school.

The Arts and Crafts movement was created by architect Augustus Pugin, along with historian John Ruskin and designer William Morris. They decried industrialisation and mass production, which they believed had affected the decorative arts, and advocated traditional craftsmanship and non-industrial production methods. They used medieval, romantic and folk art styling. The pre-Raphaelite brotherhood had a similar ethos and many studied at the Birmingham School of Art.

The school building is constructed in red brick and terracotta according to the late Victorian Arts and Crafts genre. The stained-glass lancet windows and rose roundel with a leaf motif follow neo-Gothic design principles and the depictions of lilies and sunflowers in the glazed tile insets display typical William Morris influence.

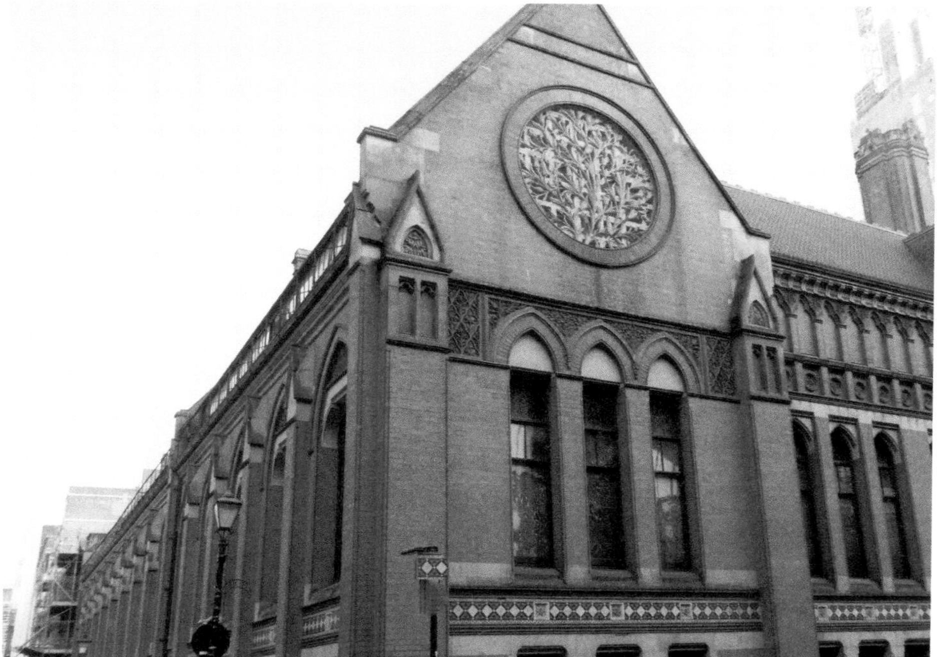

The Arts and Crafts movement and pre-Raphaelite brotherhood began here.

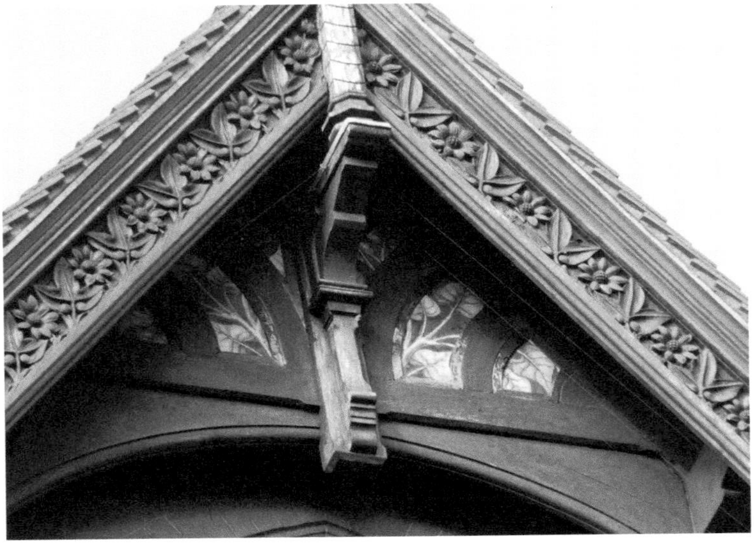

Tile inserts have a William Morris design.

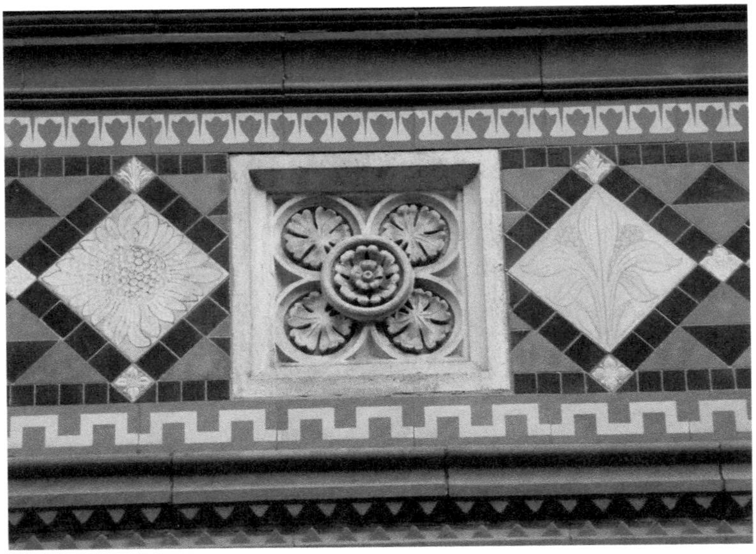

Terracotta detailing has been carefully cleaned and restored.

The building has five bays with gables and all differ, making the building non-symmetrical, although the iron railings, which are original, and the tiled friezes give an appearance of consistency. Stone pilasters reach up to an impressive first floor gable window, which has a decorative purpose as most of the natural light is provided through the skylights in the tiled roof of the studio.

The central gable has mosaic patterning, which is reflected in the interior, where all of the original mosaic floors remain. Similarly, the stained glass, metalwork and decorative wooden features date from 1885. The building was renovated in 1992, when the exterior was carefully restored to its vibrant terracotta hue.

30. Victoria Law Courts (1891)

Victoria Law Courts on Corporation Street are the largest judicial complex in Europe, with a total of twenty-two courtrooms. The building is an excellent example of terracotta neo-Gothic design and has received a Grade I listing from Historic England in recognition of its architecture.

The architects were Sir Aston Webb and Ingress Bell. When the commission to design Birmingham's new courtroom was put out to competition in 1886, the two architects submitted the best design in a field of 126 others. The foundation stone was laid by Queen Victoria in 1887 as part of her Golden Jubilee celebrations. She was so impressed by the proposal for the new courts that the architects were asked to design both the Victoria and Albert Museum and remodel the façade of Buckingham Palace. A statue of the queen for whom they were named was unveiled over the main entrance as part of the grand opening ceremony of the Victoria Law Courts in 1891.

Entrance to the building is through an arched entrance porch, flanked on either side with intricately decorated turrets and protected by the inverted portcullis, which is one of only two in the country that descend into the floor rather than being raised into the roof.

Victoria Law Courts, with its neo-Gothic architecture, has a Grade I listing.

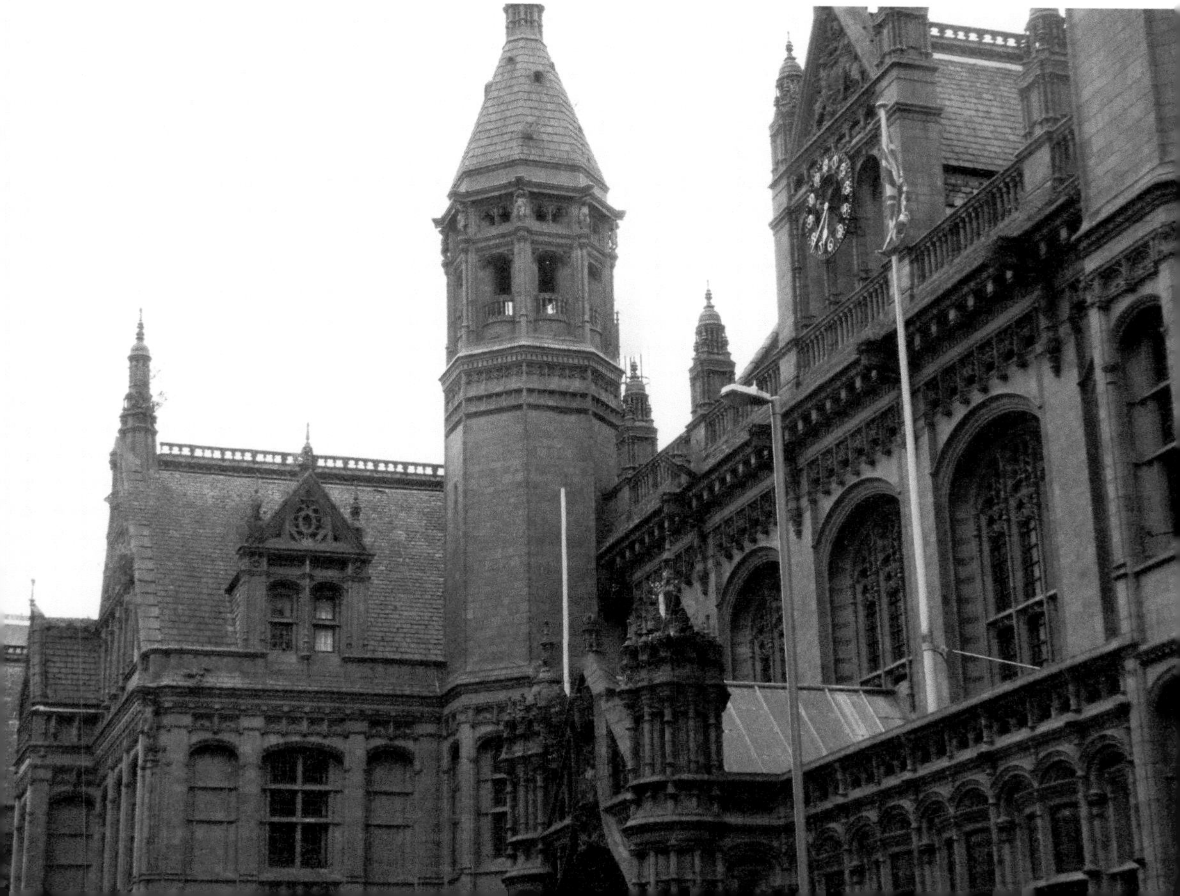

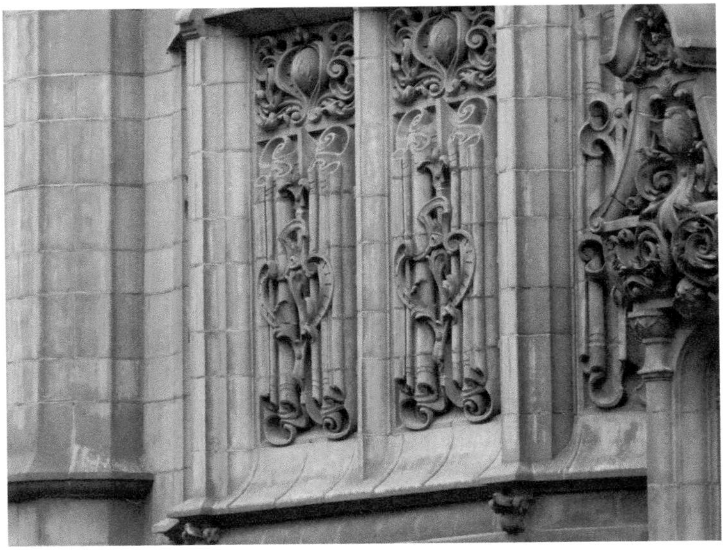

There is intricate terracotta detailing throughout the building.

The courts are an exceptional civic building, with Arts and Crafts-style detailing formed in deep red terracotta to complement the green stone tiles of the roof. The use of moulded terracotta for the façade allowed for more elaborate detailing than could have been achieved in carved stone. The interior of the building is also intricately ornamented in terracotta but contrasts the exterior by having a natural yellow hue.

The main courtrooms have features of a Tudor Revivalist style. The hammer-beam ceilings and canopy over the judge's chair are in carved dark oak to suggest medieval styling and the public balconies have been designed to resemble minstrel's galleries.

The entrance hall has round headed windows with stained-glass panels. These reflect colour onto five ostentatious chandeliers set into plasterwork ceilings bosses, which also echo an earlier age. The chandeliers were the first electric ones to be installed anywhere in the country.

31. Balsall Heath Library and Baths (1895)

The public library and baths in Balsall Heath were built on Mosely Road in 1895. The library opened first, while the baths were delayed for another decade as construction workers had difficulty boring the on-site well necessary for delivering a good water supply to the swimming pool.

The design that local architects J. Cossins and F. Peacock came up with has an eclectic red brick and terracotta configuration. The property has Flemish and Renaissance influence with Arts and Crafts motifs and has been given a Grade II listing by Historic England.

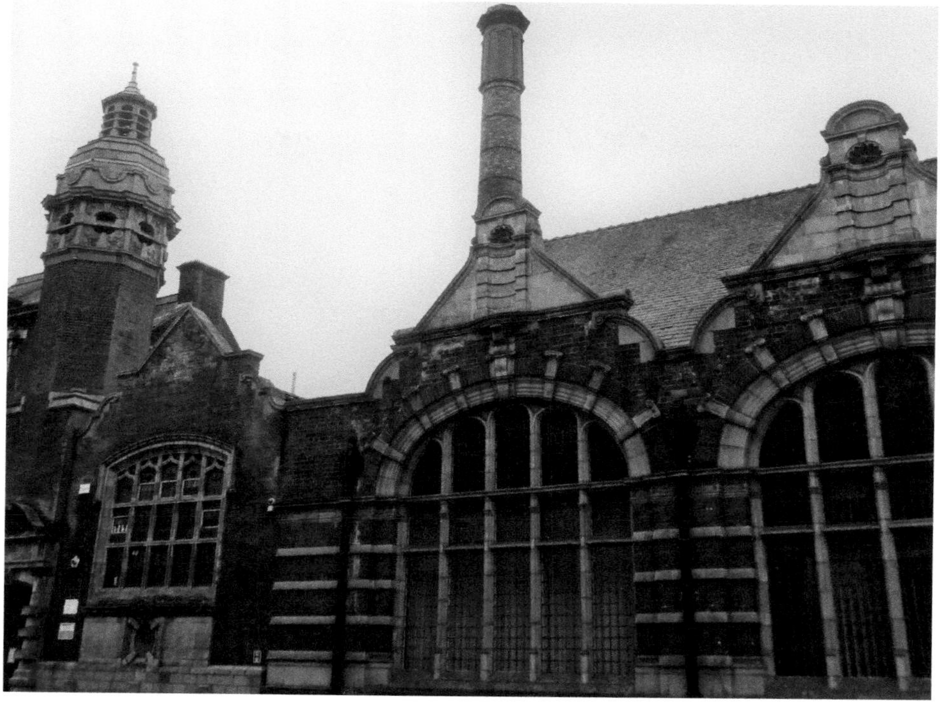

The complex remains popular with local residents.

The building is an ornate mixture of brick and cream terracotta. The main entrance of the library is at the base of a clock tower. This has a small spire with cupolas. The central entrance of the swimming baths is flanked by two octagonal towers faced in terracotta. This was the original ladies' entrance and above it is a pediment supporting a coloured sculpture of the city arms.

Gentlemen were admitted through two other entrances, one for first class and another for second class, which led into first- and second-class pool areas. The first-class pool is still in use and has most of its original fittings. There are galleries for spectators who would have had a clear view of any swimming displays put on during the pool's heyday in the early part of the twentieth century.

The sixty-four changing cubicles in the first-class pool are glazed in terracotta tiles, while the second-class pool had no changing cubicles and bathers would have changed by the poolside. There was no heating until the 1950s and before this swimming only took place between the months of March and November. In the winter months, the pool was covered with a temporary floor and used for municipal social events.

During the Second World War the pools were floored over and used as a hospital for the victims of local bombing raids. An incendiary bomb landed on the baths while it was in use as a hospital but the fire was quickly extinguished with no casualties or damage.

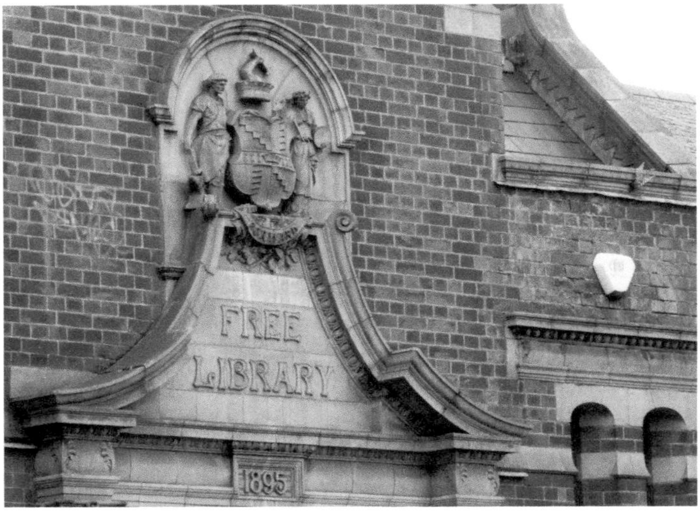

Terracotta and stone are used for the elegant detailing.

The library and its interior are also original. The most dramatic feature is a frieze depicting people absorbed in books, which surrounds the large central skylight.

32. The Red Palace, Nos 1–7 Constitution Hill (1896)

The Grade II listed building on the corner of Constitution Hill and Hampton Street is known as the Red Palace. The site is now occupied by a Middle Eastern restaurant, but when it was built in 1896, it was a factory for successful Birmingham toolmaker H. B. Sale.

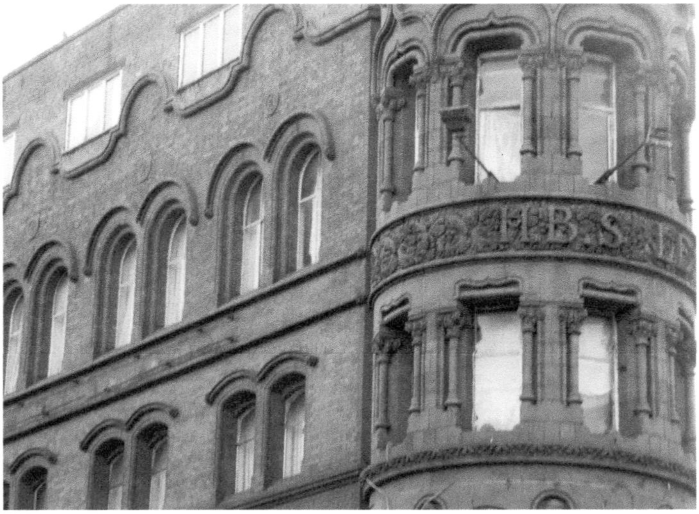

The Red Palace was built to celebrate the British Empire.

H. B. Sale had been successfully trading for over thirty years when they commissioned architects William Doubleday and James Shaw to design a factory and office block for them. The building was an interesting mixture of industrial design and also a celebration of both England's modernity and the British Empire. The Red Palace was built during the time of the English Raj in India and Eastern influence is reflected in the frontispiece tower of the property, which is reminiscent of the palaces of the Maharajahs. The tower also forms the front of the subtle triangular shape of the property. It bears a strong resemblance to the Flatiron Building in New York, which was considered to be the epitome of forward-thinking architecture and was emulated by the architects of the Red Palace.

The building was constructed in a Spanish Romanesque style in red brick with bold rows of arched windows. There are rich terracotta decorations and the name of the original occupier, H. B. Sale, is written out in floral lettering. The top floor of the property was added during Birmingham's building boom of the mid-twentieth century. This was before listing regulations to protect the integrity of the building's appearance had been put in place and contrasts in style.

H. B. Sale moved out in the early twentieth century and the property had a series of commercial uses before becoming a restaurant.

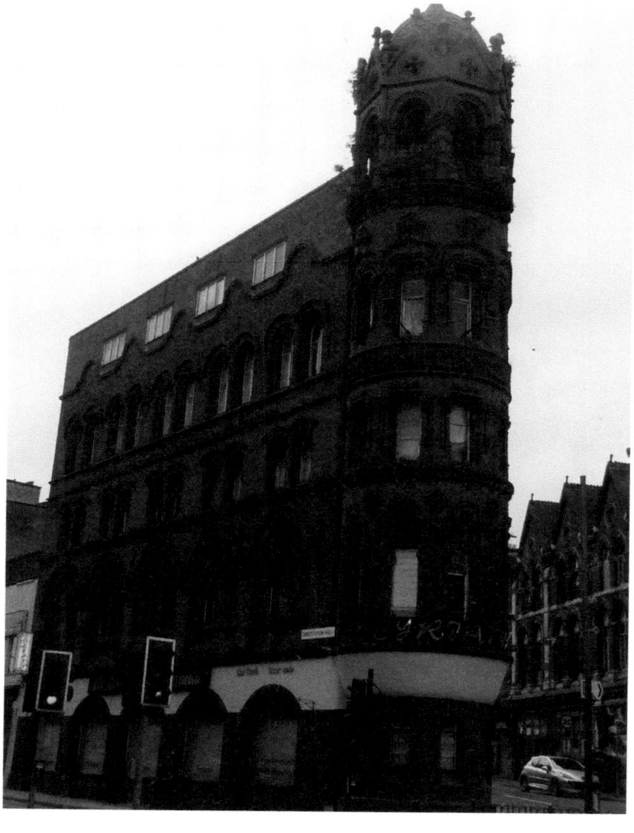

Brick and terracotta are used in the Spanish Romanesque design.

33. No. 21 Yately Road (1899)

In the whole of Birmingham just one domestic building has been granted a Grade I listing by Historic England. It was given to No. 21 Yately Road, Edgbaston, in recognition of its outstanding architectural interest.

No. 21 is the fourth in a row of Arts and Crafts-style houses designed by leading Birmingham architect Herbert Buckland. He designed it to be his personal dwelling and, after its completion in 1899, Buckland moved in and continued to live there until his death in 1951. He had studied architecture at the Birmingham School of Art and later joined the Birmingham Civic Society. As a leading member of the philanthropic society, Buckland became instrumental in many improvements to Birmingham in the 1920s. This included rehousing residents of slum clearance in new-build homes and the creation of parks and community spaces.

The exterior of No. 21 Yately Road has remained unaltered since it was built. The white painted house follows the original colour scheme with its red tile, deep hipped roof and green guttering. The property has a slightly off-centre gabled bay containing the front door. This is shielded from the weather by a slate hood that follows the lines of the arched door perfectly. The house is set in a large garden that was created by eminent garden designer Gertrude Jekyll. The layout is exactly as she designed it over a century ago and it has a wide range of unusual plants and flowers.

No. 21 Yately Road is an exceptional Arts and Crafts house.

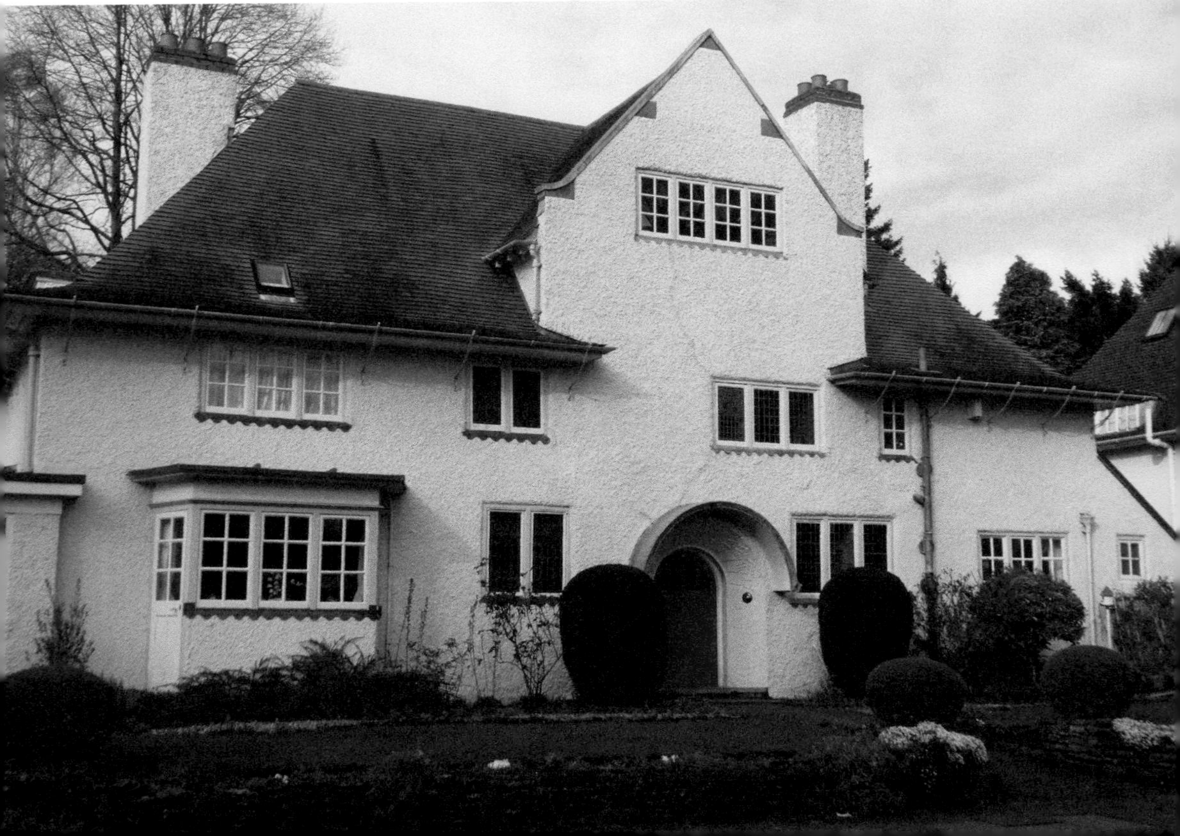

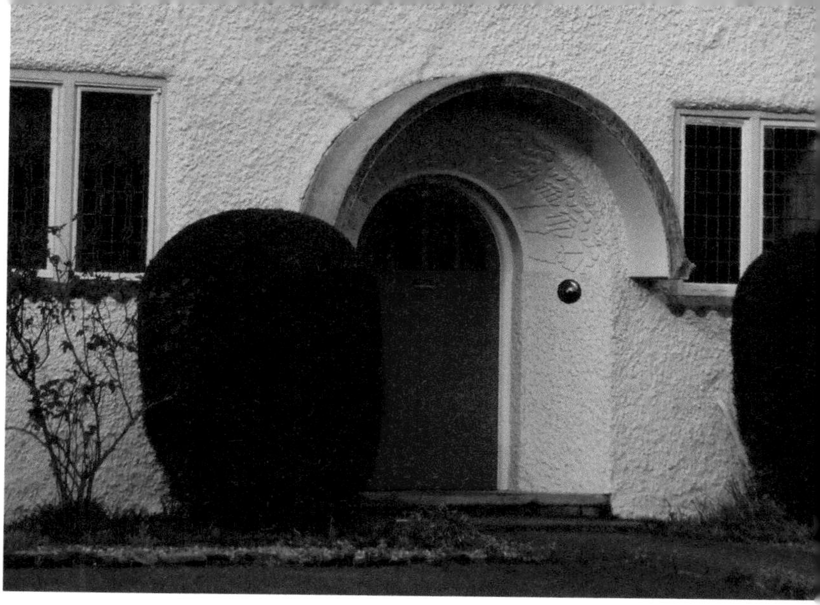
Original features of the property have been preserved.

The interior of the property is also largely untouched. The wood and brass work is of exceptional quality and was executed by local craftsmen who followed the ideals of the Arts and Crafts movement. The decorative detailing on the interior plasterwork matches the ornamentation on the copper hoods of the fireplaces and the stained-glass inserts in some of the windows were produced by William Morris.

34. Nos 122–124 Colmore Row (1900)

In eighteenth-century Birmingham, Colmore Row was a street of Georgian town houses built for wealthy manufacturers who had recently moved into the area. When the lease on the row expired in the mid-nineteenth century, the brick and stucco town houses were sold as freehold and gradually demolished to be replaced by a variety of commercial premises.

The Eagle Insurance Company commissioned architects William Lethaby and Joseph Ball to design an office building for them on the site of two of the demolished houses. The building opened in 1900 with an eagle sculpture below the eaves to visually display the company name.

The property has been given a Grade I listing due to the eminence of the two architects. They were forward-thinking members of the Arts and Crafts movement and the property has been described as one of the most originally designed premises in Arts and Crafts free style. Lethaby was an early advocate of the modernist movement and the beginnings of the minimalistic style can be seen in the plain symmetrical frontage of Nos 122–124 Colmore Row. This is most evident in the middle portion of the building, which has a stone façade with evenly spaced sash windows and geometric pilasters.

The Arts and Crafts style is shown in the marble-lined doorways with their original patinated brass doors and the brick chequerboard ornamentation above the triangular and semicircular pediments. The interior retains its original plaster

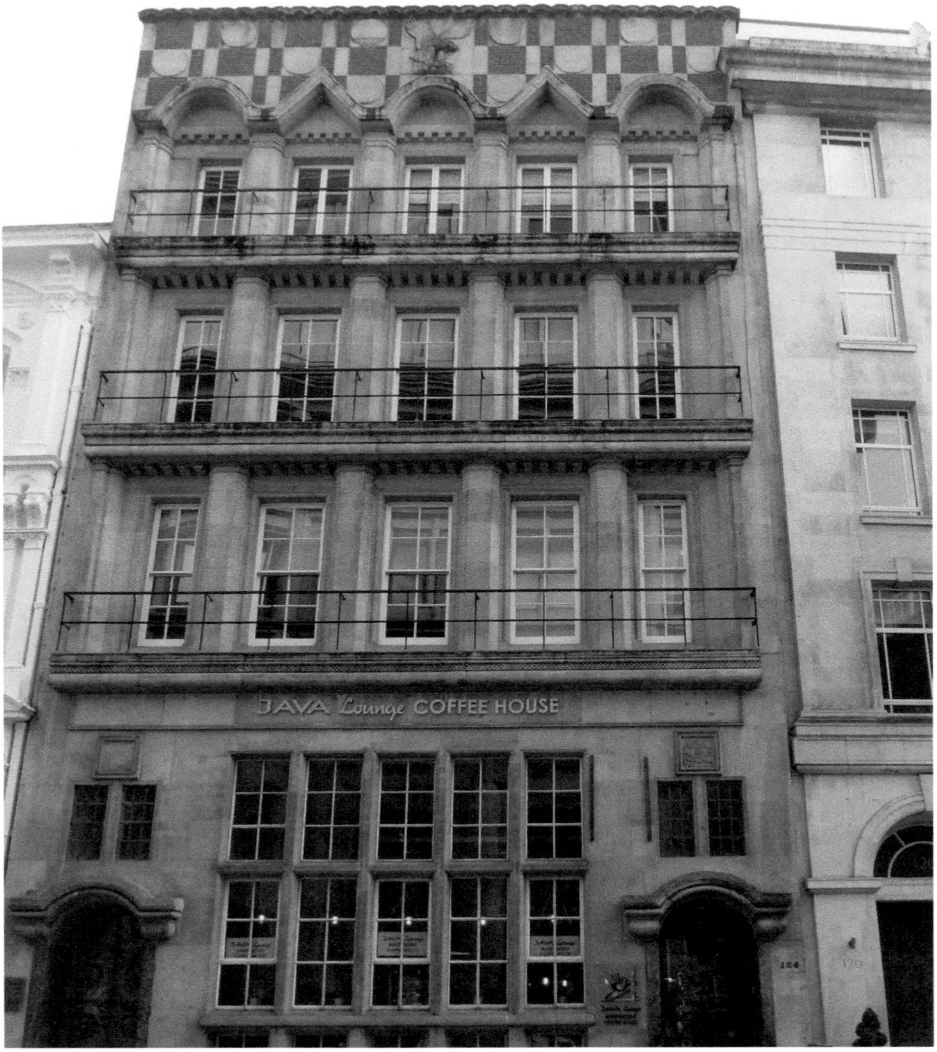

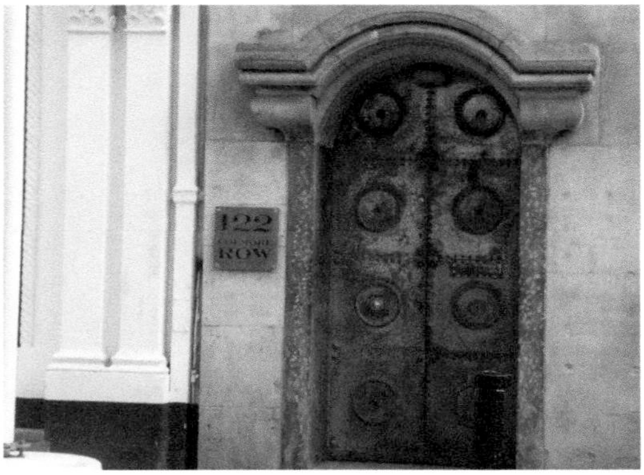

Above: Early modernist movement influence is shown in the unfussy façade.

Left: Stylised brass and marble doorways date from the year 1900.

decorations and the ceiling borders have a design of William Morris-inspired foliage. The steep stairways feature handmade curved wooden bannisters in the Arts and Crafts style. Nos 122–124 Colmore Row has been developed and altered over time and while the upper floors of the building are still office space, the ground floor has become a coffee house.

In the 1960s the building faced demolition. Herbert Manzoni, the civil engineer who devised the modernisation of Birmingham at that time, planned a ring road to replace Colmore Row but as the 1960s progressed, land prices increased and compulsory purchase orders were postponed. By 1970 the historical importance of Birmingham's older buildings was realised and many were listed by Historic England. Nos 122–124 Colmore Row was among those protected from destruction in this way.

35. Bournville Junior School and Carillon (1906)

Bournville village was created by chocolate maker George Cadbury as a model village for his factory's workforce. Many model villages were created by philanthropic industrialists in the nineteenth century to set an example to other employers of the correct welfare for their staff. The self-contained Bournville community was personally paid for by Cadbury to allow his employees to live in a clean and spacious environment with lots of services and amenities. Bournville still regularly tops polls of the nicest place to live in England.

Bournville is one of the most pleasant areas in England.

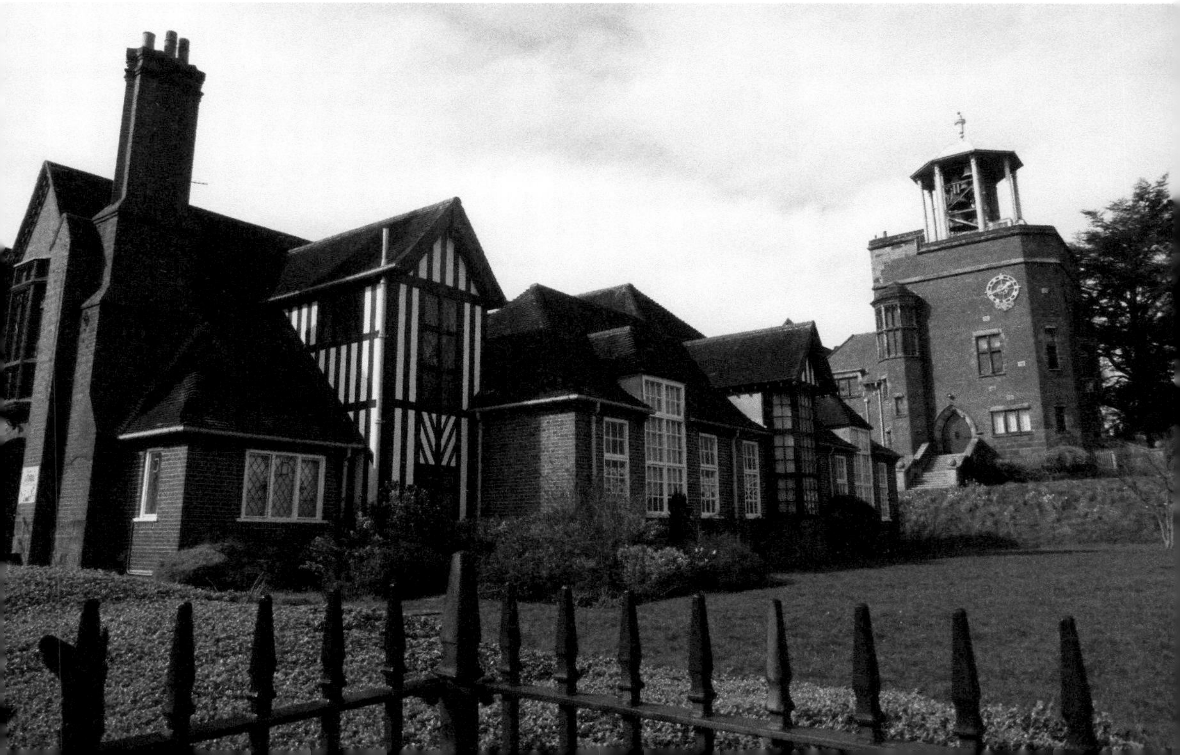

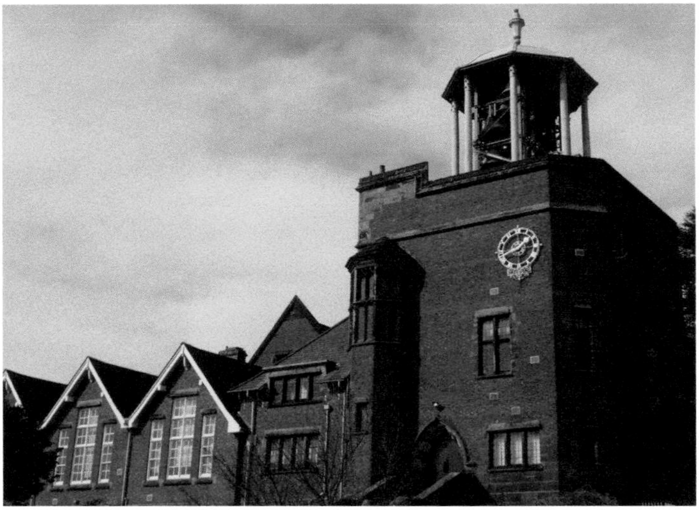

George Cadbury shared the carillon's sound with his workforce.

When the Cadbury factory relocated from the centre of Birmingham, the Bournville site was selected because George Cadbury considered the rural area would be an ideal environment for his employees to live in. He began to build a village around the new chocolate plant and architect William Alexander Harvey's designs were for Arts and Crafts-style houses, municipal leisure facilities and large parks and gardens.

Bournville Junior School, which Cadbury called his gift to Bournville, and its adjacent carillon tower were built in 1906. The school has a similar Arts and Crafts design as the workers cottages and is constructed in red brick. It has a gabled slate roof and the gable ends have the same characteristic black and white timbered detailing of the houses. The interior has original frescos by Mary Sargant Florence, who was a renowned mural artist, and there are stone friezes carved by Birmingham sculptor Benjamin Creswick.

The adjoining carillon tower is accessed by an external flight of steps and its reminiscence to a medieval keep displays the Arts and Crafts influence. The red-brick tower has oriel windows and there are gilt clock faces on adjoining sides. It is topped with an octagonal copper-clad cupola supported on eight columns and houses the largest carillon in Great Britain. The instrument had forty-eight bells that strike every quarter of an hour, and is one of the finest of its kind in the world. George Cadbury was inspired to build the carillon after he heard one play and wanted to give the melodic sound to the residents of Bournville.

36. University of Birmingham (*c.* 1908)

The University of Birmingham's campus is in Edgbaston. Over 35,000 students attend, which makes it the fourth largest university in Great Britain. It is also one of the red brick universities created in the latter years of Queen Victoria's

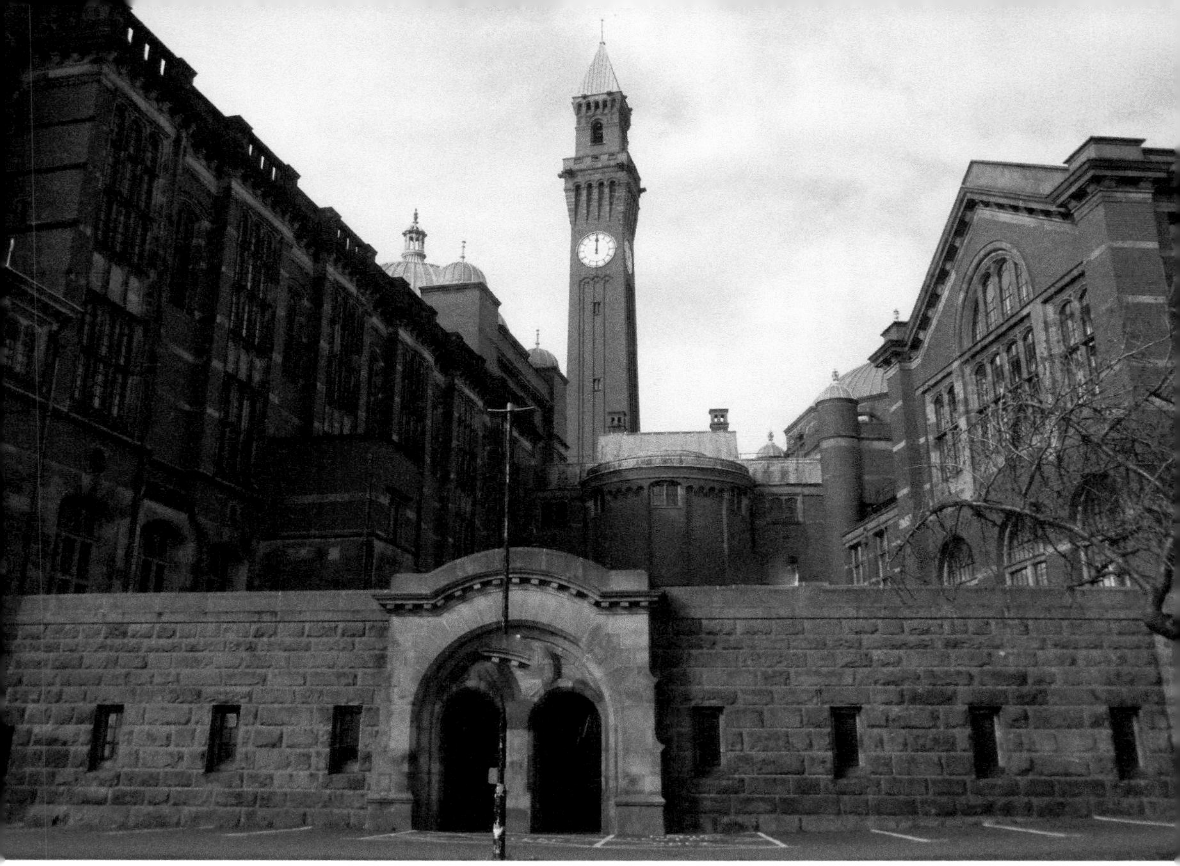

Birmingham was the first to have a civil university.

reign. These nine civic universities concentrated on practical subjects and skills rather than academia and were situated in the major industrial cities. The first of these new institutions was in Birmingham and its range of buildings were entirely constructed in red brick. When architects for the other eight universities used the same building medium, it led to them being called the red-brick universities.

Although the University of Birmingham concentrates on scientific subjects, other areas of study include Shakespeare, manuscripts of the Middle East and music. The professor of music in the early twentieth century was the eminent composer Edward Elgar.

Work on the campus began in 1900 and the first buildings, designed by Birmingham architects Aston Webb and Ingress Bell, were completed and opened in 1908. Josiah Mason, an industrialist and philanthropist, provided the money for the build. His contribution to the university has been permanently recognised in their emblem. The mermaid to the right of their heraldic shield is the symbol of the Mason family and can be seen in various locations around the campus.

An iconic feature of the University of Birmingham is the clock tower. It can be seen all across the city and is the focal point of the campus. It is officially called the Joseph Chamberlain Memorial but is known affectionately as Old Joe and at 328 feet, it is the tallest freestanding clock tower in the world.

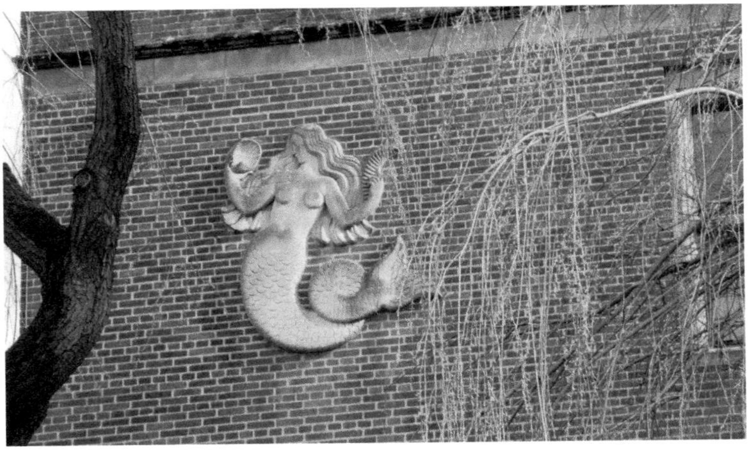

The mermaid provides an attractive university emblem.

The semicircle of buildings around the clock tower were the earliest. The red-brick halls, which have lead domed roofs and arched windows, resemble Moorish architecture and, as the university site has expanded over time, there have been many different building styles used. These include designs from the Arts and Crafts, art deco and modernist movements and more recent brutalist and postmodernist structures.

37. The Electric Theatre (1909)

The Electric is a high-quality film house on Station Street. It has been restored to its 1930s art deco appearance, but it was built in the Edwardian era. It is the earliest cinema in Great Britain that is still used for its original purpose.

The cinema was built in 1909 and seated 376 people in plush velvet tip-up seats. The thirty-minute silent show would consist of just one or two reels of celluloid with a varied theme. Comedy, drama and travelogues were the most popular and the film changed daily, encouraging customers to visit every day.

Little was left of the Edwardian Electric Theatre after the cinema was completely remodelled and extended in 1937. An attractive art deco façade was added, which had cream faience tiling with green borders. The entrance lobby was made from a coloured structural glass called Vitrolite and covered with a chrome canopy.

It was converted to a two-screen cinema in the early 1980s where it began showing 'adult' films on one screen and mainstream movies on the other before gradually losing trade and falling into disrepair.

When the cinema was renovated in the mid-1990s, it lost its art deco features and a controversial artwork by sculptor John Buckley was placed in its entrance. The sculpture was called *Thatcher's Children*, and portrayed child poverty. However, both this and the art-house films shown proved unpopular and the cinema was soon sold again.

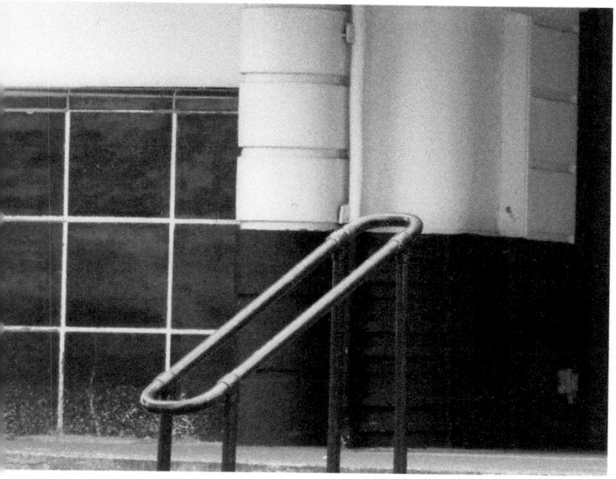

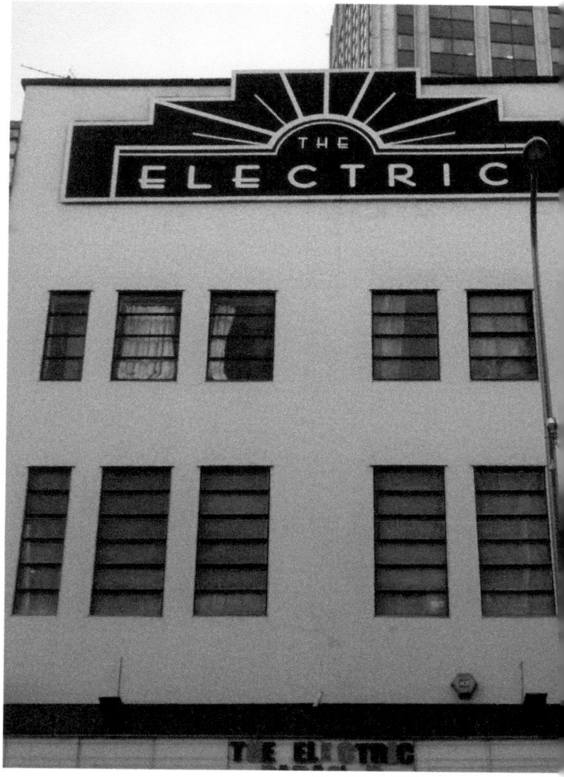

Above: Art deco monochrome features were a later addition.

Right: The Electric Theatre is an Edwardian cinema.

It was only in 2004 that the Electric Theatre regained its name, appearance and reputation when an extensive refit and restoration was undertaken by the new owners. Although all original features had been lost over the years, the exterior was painted to reflect its art deco heritage and the refitted interior is in an art deco style. The Electric is now a successful independent cinema in a regenerated area of the city centre.

38. Fort Dunlop (1916)

Fort Dunlop is a large art deco building on a site at the side of the M6 motorway. The industrial unit has become the landmark boundary of the greater Birmingham area and stands as testament to the city's heritage in manufacturing.

The Dunlop Rubber Company was founded by Birmingham man John Dunlop in 1889 and in 1916, the company built a tyre factory in the Erdington area. The main building on the site became known as Fort Dunlop and the upper floors were used as offices while the lower floor was a large storage area for the new tyres.

Fort Dunlop became the largest factory in the world and by the 1950s it employed over 10,000 people. Production ceased in the late twentieth century and, after standing empty for some years, it has now been redeveloped as business units and a hotel.

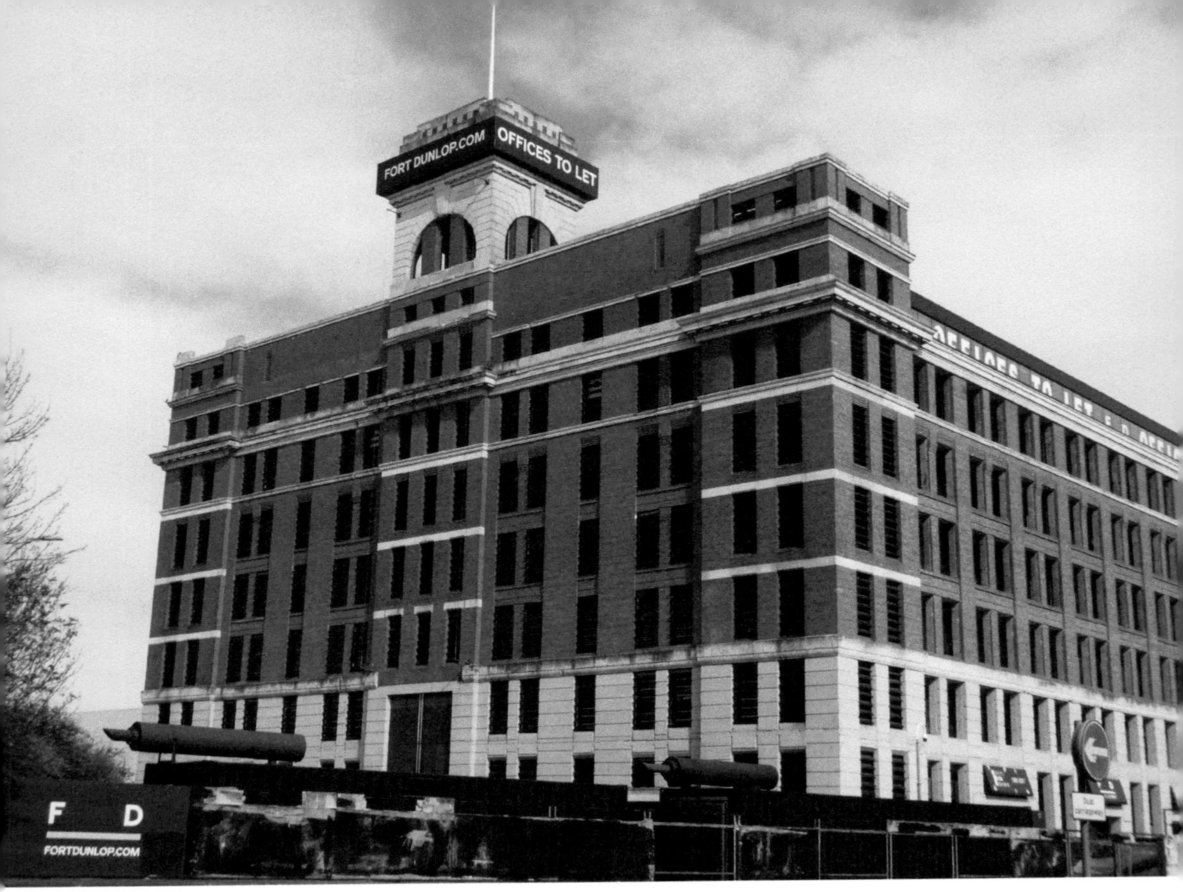

In the 1950s, Fort Dunlop was the world's largest factory.

Fort Dunlop was constructed with a concrete-clad steel frame and faced with brick and stone. Such a large manufacturing site was vulnerable to air raids during the Second World War, but despite suffering some bomb damage the exterior of the building is mostly original. It has some fine art deco features including the short central tower with the arched decoration typical of its architect, Sidney Stott.

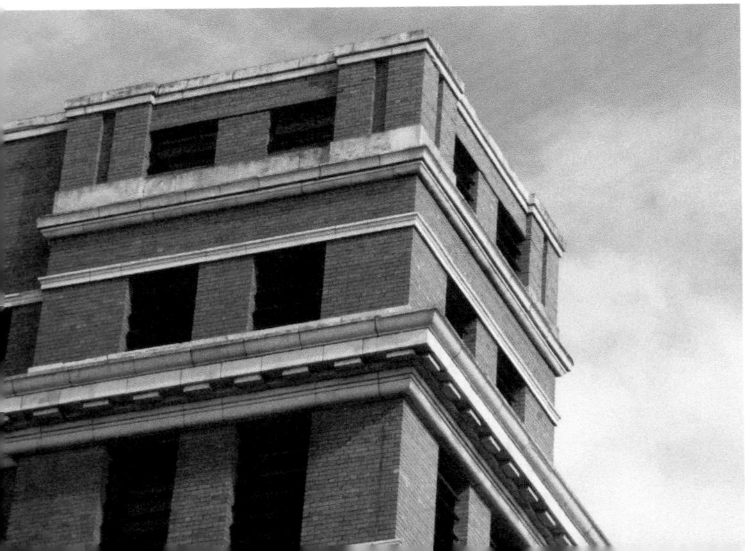

Subtle art deco styling makes this an iconic building.

Stott was well known for his industrial architecture and designed and built many mills and factories in his native Lancashire. The building has a Grade A local listing, which protects it from unsympathetic alterations.

Fort Dunlop was just one of many major producers in industrial Birmingham. HP Sauce, Typhoo Tea and Bird's Custard Powder were also local companies who became worldwide brands. Although these products are no longer manufactured in the city, the brands that were created in Birmingham are still an integral part of British culture.

39. Hall of Memory (1925)

The Hall of Memory stands as a tribute to the Birmingham citizens who fell in war and conflict. Historic England have given the monument a Grade I listing and describe it as an unusual and ambitious architectural memorial. It was opened in 1925 in remembrance of more than 12,000 people who died in the First World War.

In the early 1920s, Birmingham City Council purchased the site on which the Hall of Memory is built. The area was then an industrial canal basin and the proposal was to fill it in and create a municipal square. The plans that they drew up were in the form of a Roman-style quadrangle and included a library, concert hall, council offices and museum. The first part of the square was completed in 1925 and included the Hall of Memory. The building scheme continued until the outbreak of the Second World War but was left uncompleted. The council offices were built in the 1970s and the concert halls were completed a decade later. The library was rebuilt in 2013 and the square now has an eclectic mix of architectural styles. The area was named Centenary Square in 1989 in recognition of Birmingham having had city status for a hundred years.

The Hall of Memory was designed by Birmingham architects S. N. Cooke and W. N. Twist as an octagon with decorative Doric features. It has been built using white Portland stone and Welsh slate for the domed roof. The construction was

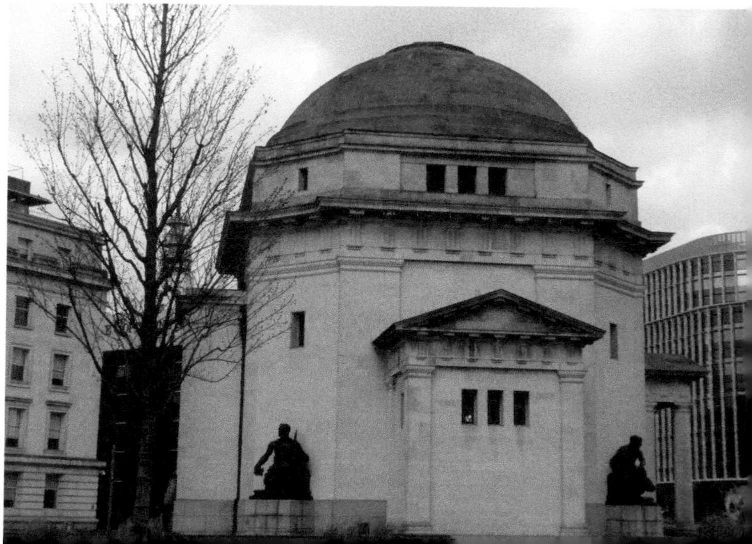

The Hall of Memory honours those who died in war.

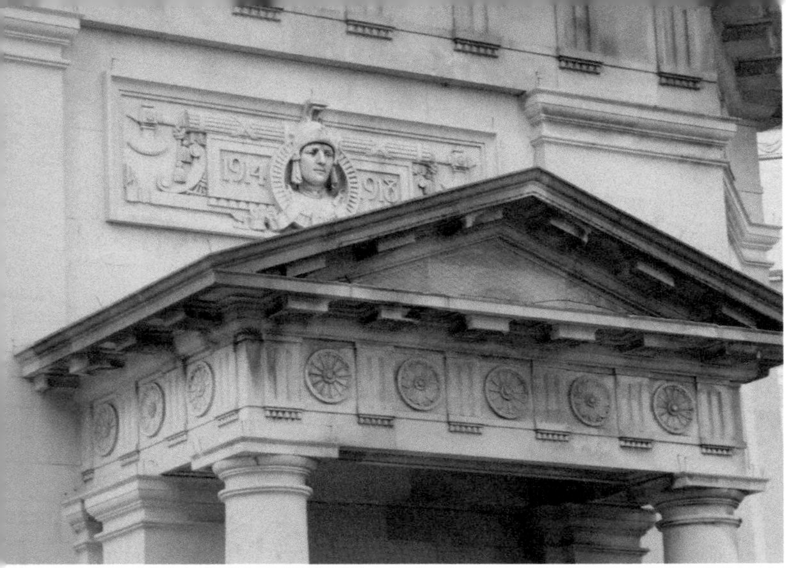

Doric porticos have highly decorative features.

completed by local craftsmen and, as the £60,000 needed to build the memorial was financed from public donations, The Hall of Memory became a tribute to Birmingham residents by Birmingham residents.

Four statues alternate with porticos around the memorial and these were created by Birmingham sculptor Albert Toft. They depict the British Army, the Royal Navy, Women's Services and the RAF. Inside the building are three bas-relief plaques designed by William Bloye. They represent life in armed service and are entitled *The Call, Front Line* and *Return*. A stained-glass window by Richard Stubington lights the interior, where a marble podium supports a wood and glass casket containing rolls of honour from the First World War and subsequent conflicts.

40. Odeon Cinema (1935)

On Kettlehouse Road, in the Kingstanding area of Birmingham, is a stunning art deco Odeon cinema. When it received its Grade II listing from Historic England, they described it as one of the best surviving examples of an Odeon cinema in Great Britain. The Odeon cinema chain was owned by entertainment mogul Oscar Deutsch and the name was reputed to be an acronym for Oscar Deutsch Entertains Our Nation. However, 'odeon' is the ancient Greek word for theatre and the more likely derivation.

The Odeon cinemas Deutsch constructed followed the same distinctive design. They had curved theatre frontages, highly glazed tiling, a prominent tower and normally had an asymmetrical plan for maximum interest. The Kingstanding Odeon mostly conforms to this design but unusually, it is symmetrical. There was originally a plan by Deutsch's architect, Birmingham-born Harry Weedon, to mount a spotlight on the top of the tower but this was never realised.

The cinema was built to provide entertainment for the new Kingstanding estate, which was begun in 1928. There were 4,000 new homes built on the site and it was the largest ever interwar municipal housing development.

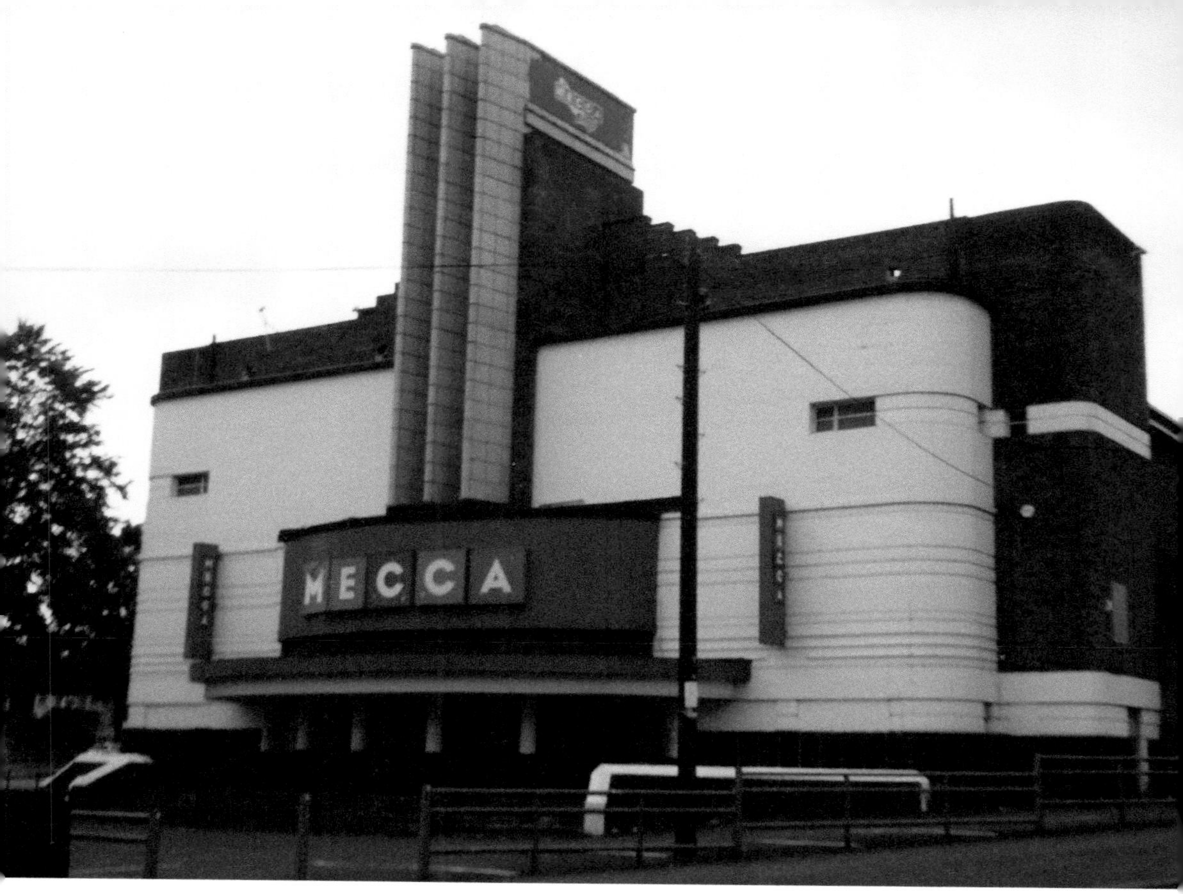

Kingstanding's Odeon cinema is one of the best-preserved examples of art deco.

The cinema had its opening night in July 1935 and the first film shown was *The Lives of a Bengal Lancer*, starring Gary Cooper. The Odeon continued to enthral audiences for twenty-seven years until it closed in 1962. Since that time the largely unchanged building has been used as a bingo hall.

The Odeon is a striking building with original exterior railings leading up to the main front doors, which are also original. The three-fin tower still dominates the

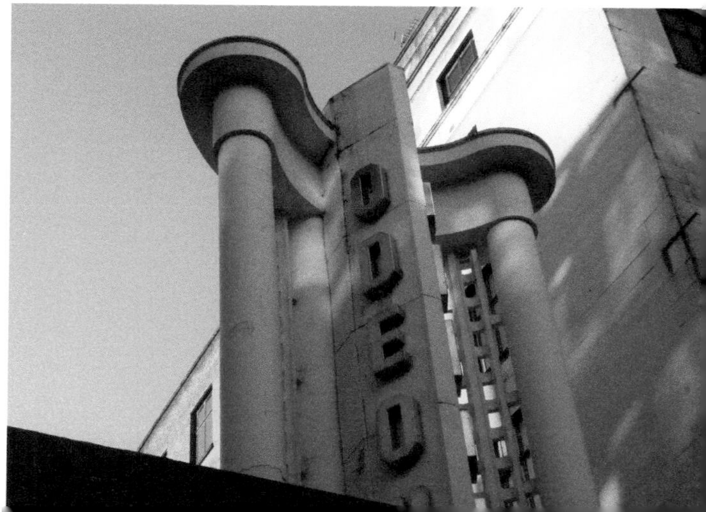

Odeon cinemas were renowned for their modernity and stylishness.

skyline and, where the original lettering spelled out Odeon, this has now been altered to reflect the building's current use. The cinema was constructed using white painted brick and produces a monochrome effect against the highly glazed black tiling.

The interior was intentionally plain to prevent the patron from being distracted from the film and the auditorium retains its subtle decoration. Art deco grilles still line the walls and large geometric light units survive under the later dropped ceiling.

41. Barber Institute of Fine Arts (1939)

The Barber Institute of Fine Arts is an art gallery and concert hall on the campus of the University of Birmingham. It was built specifically for the historical study of fine art and is the legacy of Dame Martha Constance Barber.

Sir Henry and Martha Barber were a wealthy society couple with a love for fine art. They wanted to create a museum or gallery in Birmingham to share this appreciation with their home city, but Henry died before any firm plans were made. In 1932, Dame Martha founded the Barber Institute in memory of her late husband. She decided to create an educational art collection that was of the quality seen in the Wallace collection or the national gallery. When she passed away, she left her entire estate to the accumulation of artworks and the construction of a building in which to house them.

The Barber Institute now has major collections by Van Gogh, Monet, Turner, Botticelli, Rubens and Rossetti. It has one of the largest coin collections in the

The institute has collections by Van Gogh, Monet and Turner.

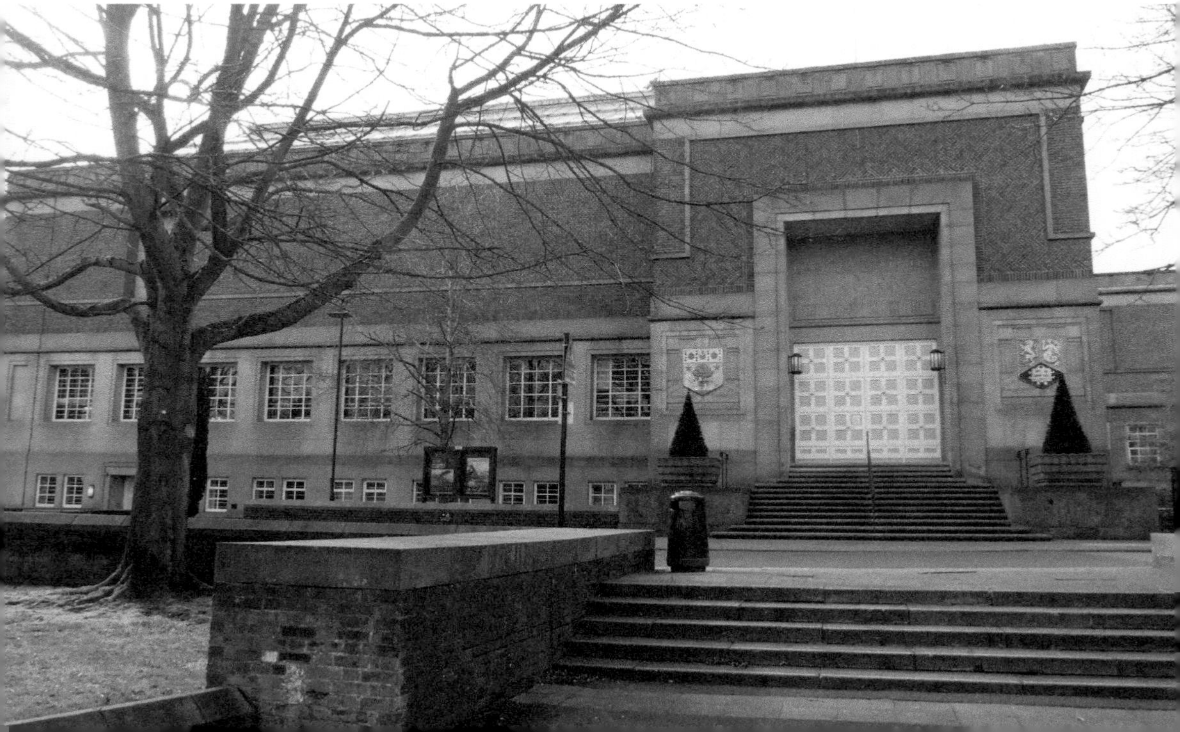

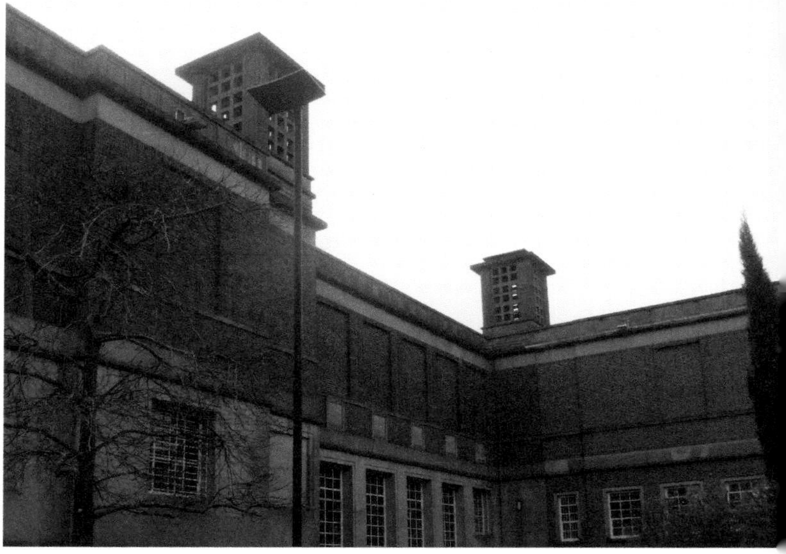

Geometric simplicity is evidence of the art deco styling.

world and houses an important music library. Concerts and music festivals are held regularly in the concert hall.

A suitable building was required to house such priceless works and architect Robert Atkinson, who was a major name in art deco building design, was commissioned to build it. When the gallery opened in 1939, it was heralded as a masterpiece in institutional design and has since been described as expressing the true spirit of 1930s English architecture.

The Barber Institute of Fine Arts has been given a Grade II listing by Historic England. The building is influenced by the classical style and is constructed in brick and stone. Its design is sharp and linear and the horizontal plane is accentuated by the lack of windows on the upper floor. Decoration is added by contrasting the colours of the brick and stone layers and edging the roof with a balustrade. There is a geometric design element in the flues and this is mirrored in the door surrounds of the main entrance.

Inside, the lower floor consists of a large concert hall surrounded by lecture halls and libraries, while the first floor contains galleries displaying the many art collections.

42. Wake Green Prefabs (1945)

After the Second World War there was a housing crisis in most of Great Britain and the city of Birmingham was no exception. The desperate need to re-home the victims of bomb damage brought about the Temporary Housing Programme, a government scheme to build half a million new homes as quickly and cheaply as possible. A system was devised where frames were erected and clad with prefabricated sheets, taking only around forty hours to complete.

The row of sixteen prefabricated bungalows on Wake Green Road, Moseley, are Grade II listed and were erected in 1945. The specific model of steel framed home

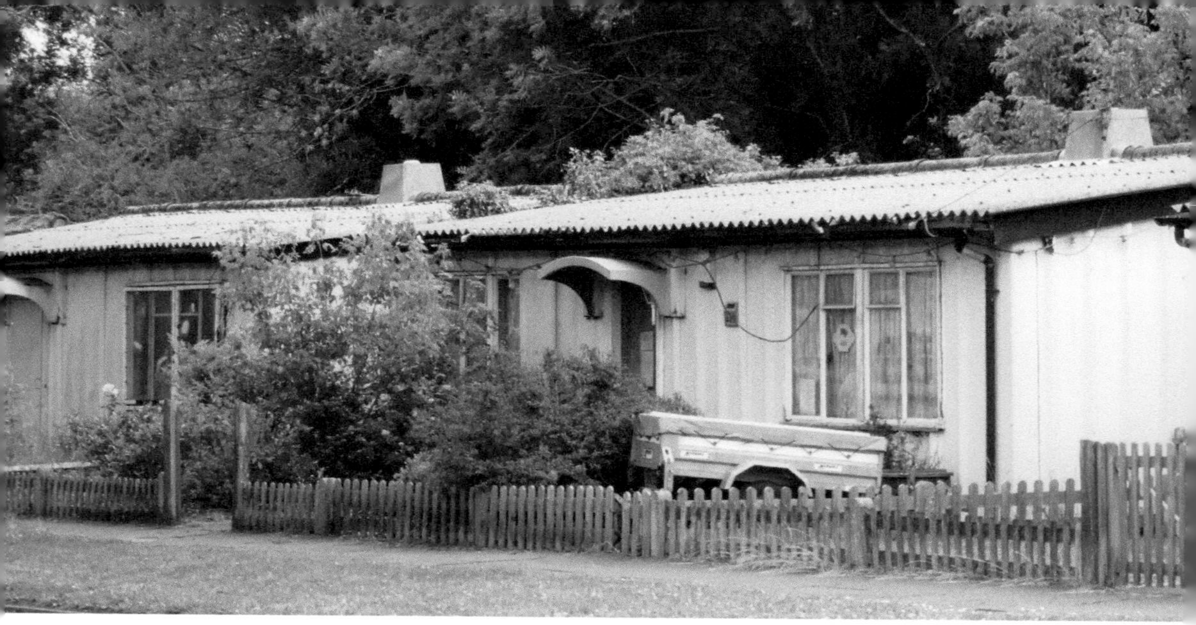

Although built to be temporary, the bungalows have proved durable.

is known as the Phoenix and each cost £12,000 to build. As the average price of a home just prior to the war had been £750, the aim of the Temporary Housing Programme to provide cheap accommodation was not entirely met. However, the money was well spent as the prefabs all had two bedrooms and lounge, a fully fitted bathroom, separate indoor toilet, central heating and kitchens fitted out with modern labour-saving gadgets like washing machines. They also had a large garden with a private shed and became known as the palaces for the people.

The prefabs were only expected to last for ten years and it was originally planned to gradually replace the exteriors with bricks and mortar and create permanent homes. However, this never happened and most prefabs soon succumbed to rot and rust, or were demolished as the new high-rise social housing schemes began.

The Wake Green bungalows, with their iconic curved metal porches, were well-built and have survived over half a century longer than expected. Birmingham

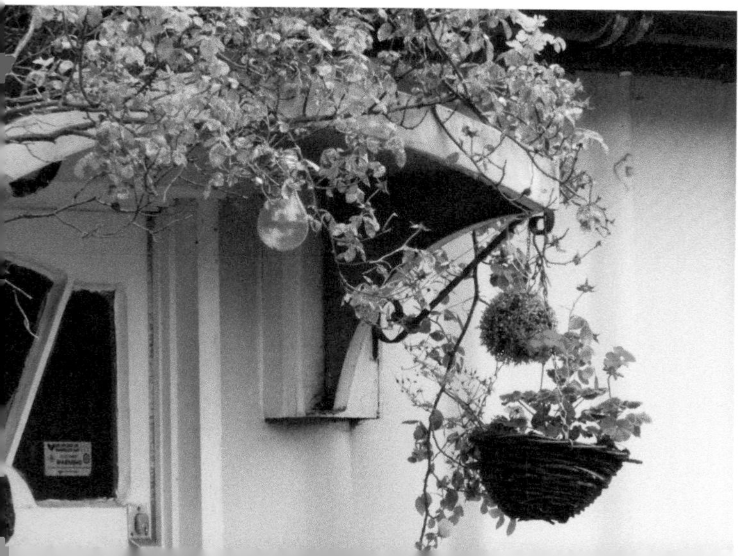

The prefabs were called the palaces for the people.

City Council still own ten of the homes and they have altered very little since they were built. Some still have the original colour scheme of magnolia emulsion and green gloss and have retained their 'English cottage' character.

Campaigns by their residents have saved the prefabs from demolition more than once and they were finally listed by Historic England due to their insight into post-war social housing.

43. The Rotunda (1965)

The Rotunda has become the most iconic Birmingham landmark. The Grade II listed structure is 226 feet tall and was designed by Birmingham architect James Roberts as an office block and shop units for the major post-war regeneration of Birmingham.

The original design of the twenty-five-floor building included a cinema and a revolving restaurant but neither were completed. Construction took three years and it opened in 1965 to negative reviews from other architects. However, the population of Birmingham saw it in a better light and viewed the Rotunda with affection.

By the 1980s there were plans to modernise the area and it was suggested that the Rotunda be demolished to make way for a new building. Birmingham residents and supporters of twentieth-century architecture mounted a campaign to save the building and succeeded when, in 2000, it was granted listed status. Historic England recognised it for its straightforward form, which exemplified the move towards simpler shapes in architecture in the 1960s.

This can be seen in its uncomplicated structure of a reinforced concrete core and exterior walls consisting almost entirely of textured glass. The podium from which the Rotunda rises contains retail units and bars and in 2008, the upper storeys were converted into 232 luxury apartments. These were so popular with residents that the final release of ninety-two sold in just three hours.

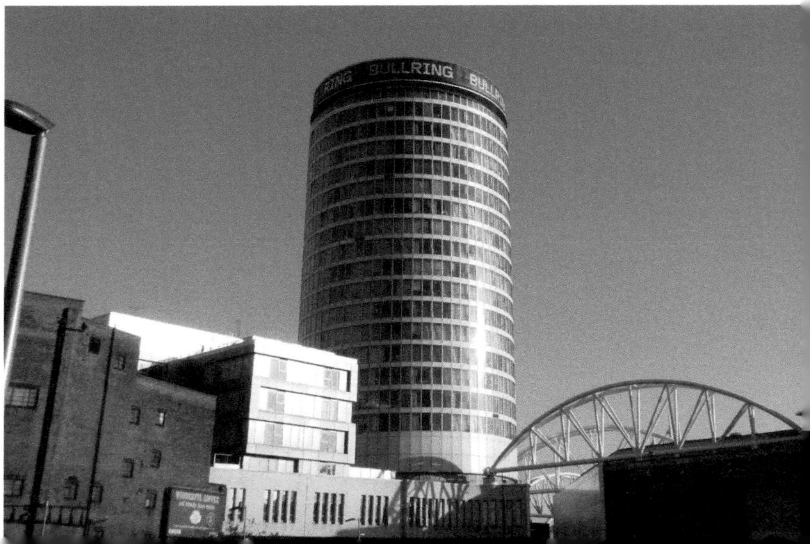

Birmingham's iconic building is 226 feet tall.

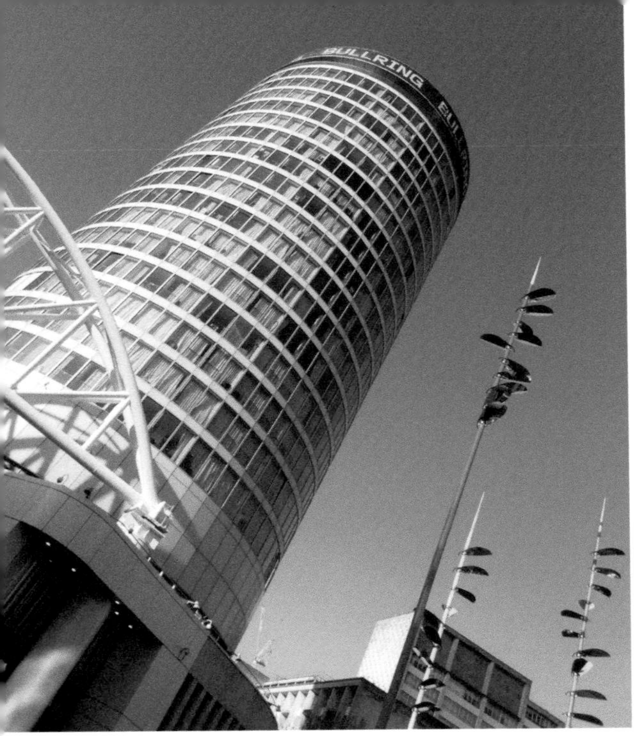

The Rotunda has become highly sought-after luxury apartments.

When the Rotunda first opened it included a textured concrete mural by award-winning Birmingham artist John Poole. The artwork was on the central interior column and reached up for many storeys. The mural has been preserved and is now in a retail unit where it is safely hidden by the interior shop fittings.

44. BT Tower (1966)

The BT Tower on Lionel Street has been a distinctive part of the Birmingham cityscape since it opened in 1966. With a height of nearly 500 feet, it is the tallest structure in Birmingham and took three years to build.

It was part of a nationwide network of telecommunication relays for telephone, radio and television. The eighty microwave dishes used for transmissions from the structure proved to be far more efficient than the previous aerial, which had been on nearby Telephone House.

The BT Tower was first known as the Post Office Tower when it was designed by the Ministry of Public Buildings and Works. Originally, it was to have been round like the Post Office Tower in London but the final design was square as it was considered to be more aesthetically pleasing. The proposed height of 600 feet would have created problems for incoming aircraft to Birmingham Airport and the architectural design was therefore adjusted to be shorter but wider in diameter to allow for all of the equipment to be installed.

The tower has twenty-six storeys full of equipment and, although some of the instruments are now obsolete, they have not been removed and provide an interesting

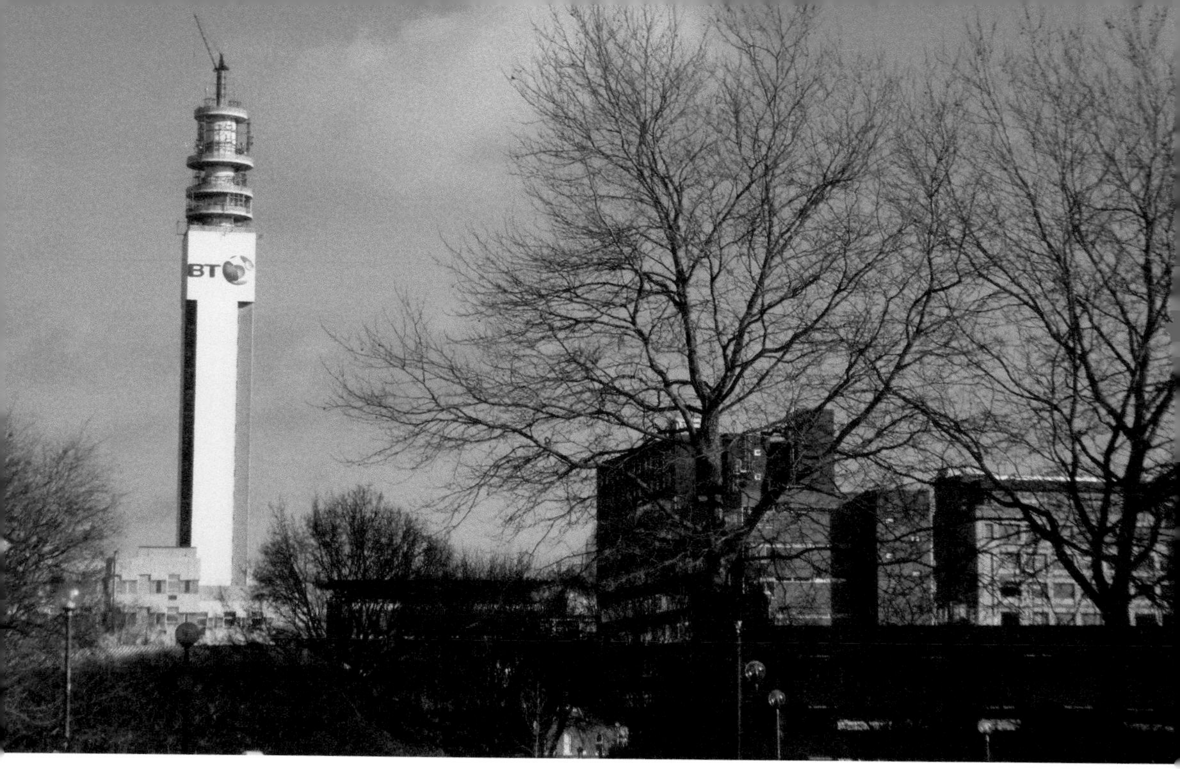

Above: Birmingham's skyline is dominated by the BT Tower.

Right: Peregrine falcons regularly nest among the aerials and microwave dishes.

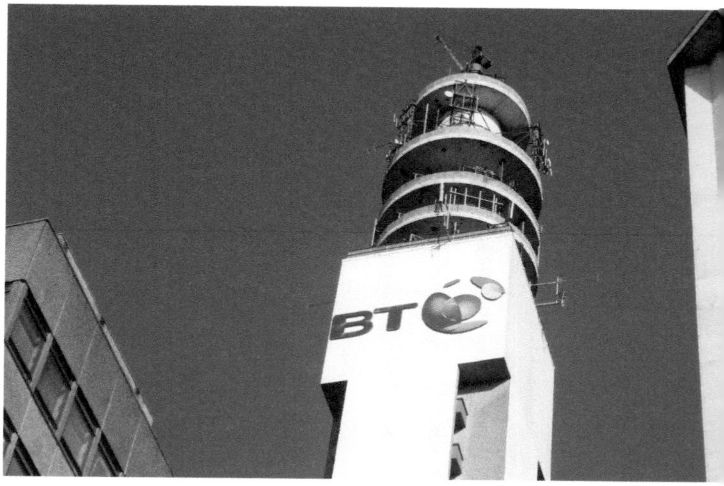

insight into electronic history. The crane on the top of the landmark is constantly used to correctly position the transmission dishes on the five aerial galleries.

The BT Tower is made of concrete and has articulated corners to prevent sway. This movement is caused by wind resistance and may disrupt communications; however, it does not deter a pair of peregrine falcons that have regularly nested on the twenty-second floor of the structure. Since 2010, they have had their own 'peregrine cam', which live streams their movements and that of their chicks to a large and fascinated audience.

45. Our Lady Help of Christians (1967)

Our Lady Help of Christians is a stunning modern church in the Tile Cross area of Birmingham and was completed in 1967.

It was during the redevelopment of the area in the 1950s and 1960s, which included the construction of some of Birmingham's first high rise blocks, that many building site workers from Ireland settled in the community. There was only an Anglican church in the district at that time and building a place of worship for the Catholic faith became a priority.

The new church was Our Lady Help of Christians. It was built in a brutalist style to a design by Richard Gilbert Scott. The architect was the great-grandson of the prolific designer of Gothic Revival churches in the nineteenth century, Sir George Gilbert Scott. The 1960s design has been awarded a Grade II listing as it has a unique appearance and also because of the quality of workmanship and interior fittings.

The high altar commands a central position in the cruciform building. It has been made of simple white marble blocks and has a backdrop of stained glass. Artist John Chrestien was a college contemporary of the architect and provided Our Lady of Help with its magnificent stained glass. He produced the glasswork in a limited

Oxidised copper cladding gives a stylised nature to the church.

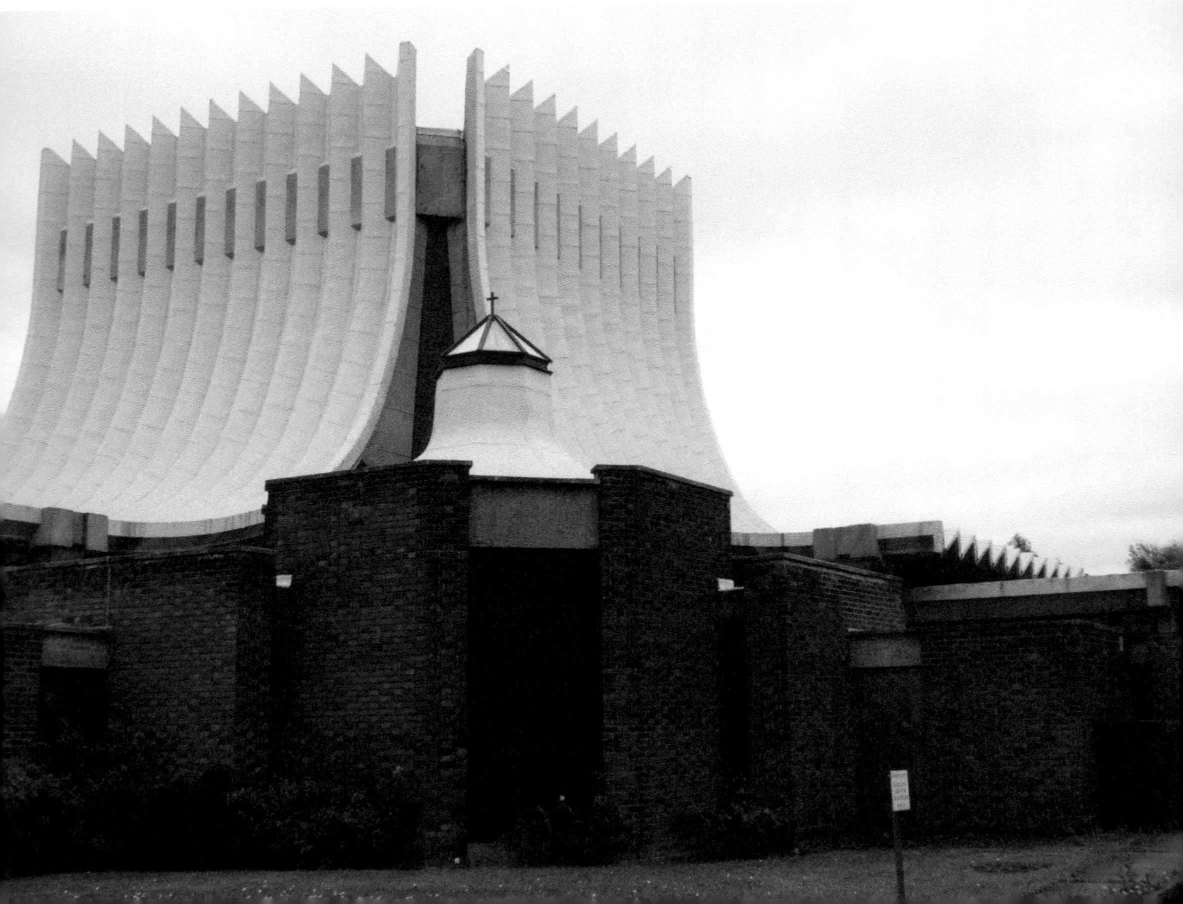

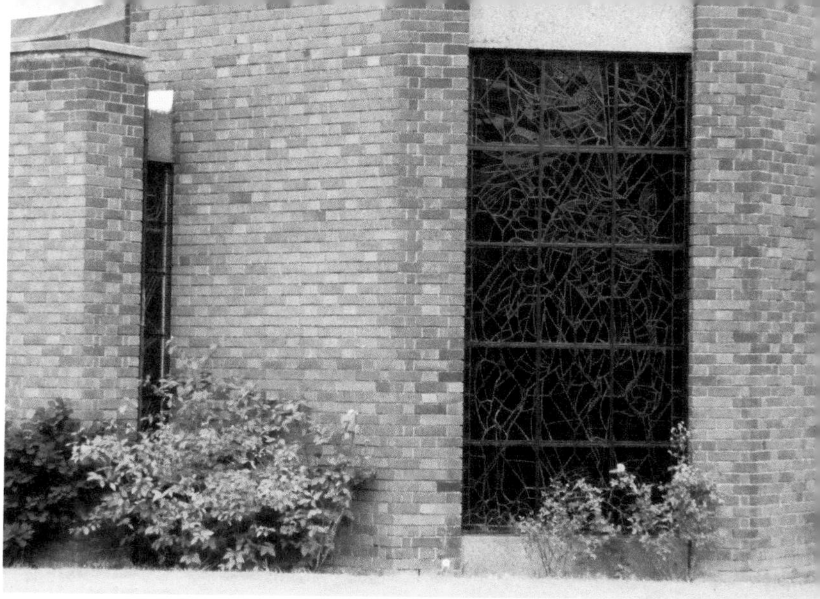

A limited range of colours adds impact to the glass.

range of colours and the use of mainly blue, black and red in clear windows has given more impact to his designs while allowing light to flood the nave. The aisle is flanked by rows of simple bench pews, which have all been crafted from solid timber. The wooden interior doors also have brass fittings made by local craftsmen.

The reinforced concrete ribs that curve upwards to a low central tower are visible both internally and externally. They are clad in copper and their serrated edges give the church its unique appearance. Although the copper has oxidised to become green, this does not detract from the appearance of the church. The bell-shaped roof of the baptistry and that of the lady chapel also share this copper cladding.

46. Gravelly Hill Interchange – Spaghetti Junction (1972)

The Gravelly Hill area of Birmingham is the site of a massive feat of concrete building work. The structure is officially called the Gravelly Hill Interchange, although it is always called by its nickname, Spaghetti Junction. Opinions on the architectural merit of the road system are divided. Its proponents call it monumental while it is described by opposers as monstrous.

In Birmingham, the 1960s were a time of economic growth and development and there were plans to completely remodel the city. More trade and housing meant more vehicles, and the Aston Expressway was built to join the city centre with nearby motorways. The Department of Transport was also looking into a method to link the M1 and M6 and a giant intersection at Gravelly Hill, incorporating the A38, was the solution.

When it opened in 1972, a journalist on *The Birmingham Evening Mail* wrote, 'the junction is a cross between a plate of spaghetti and a bad attempt at knot tying.' The article went to press under the title 'Spaghetti Junction' and the name stuck.

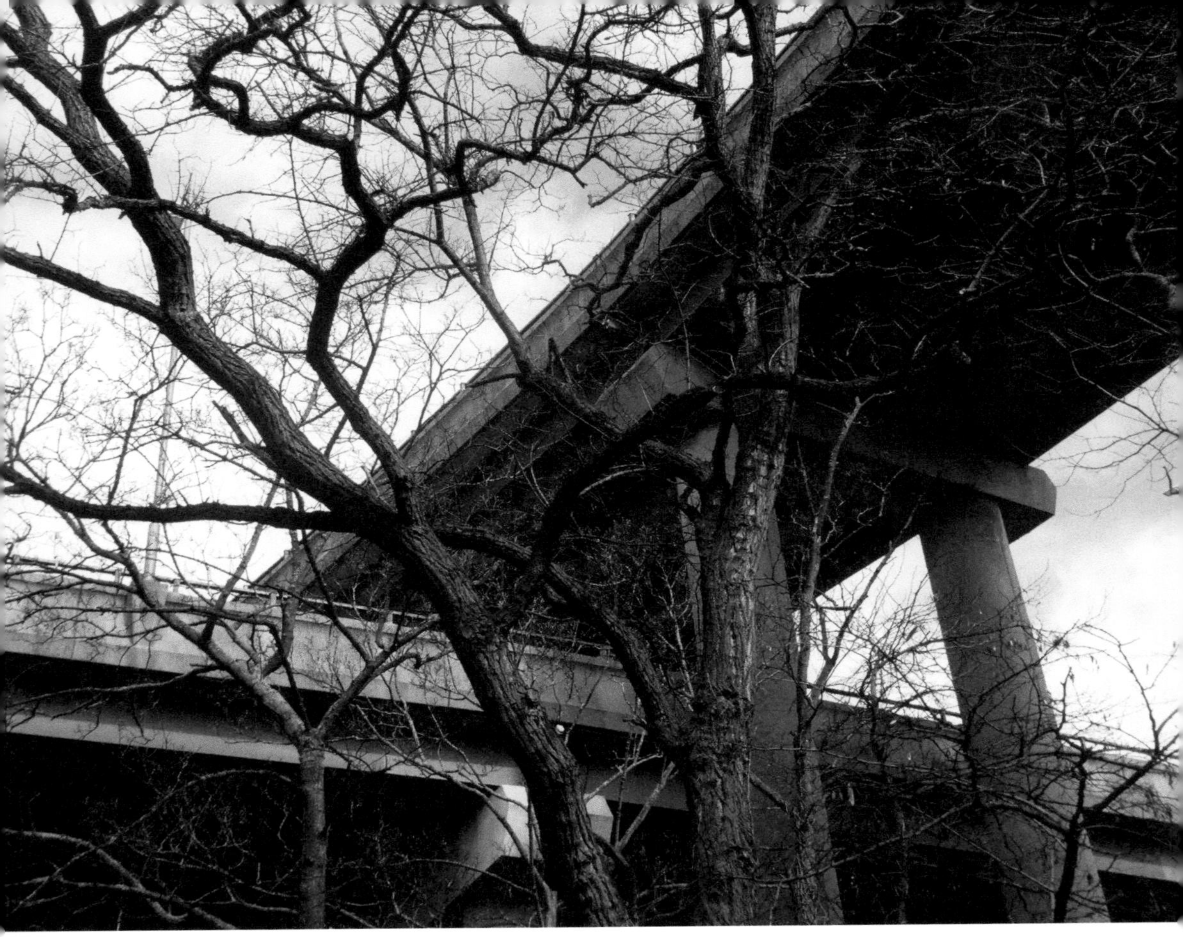

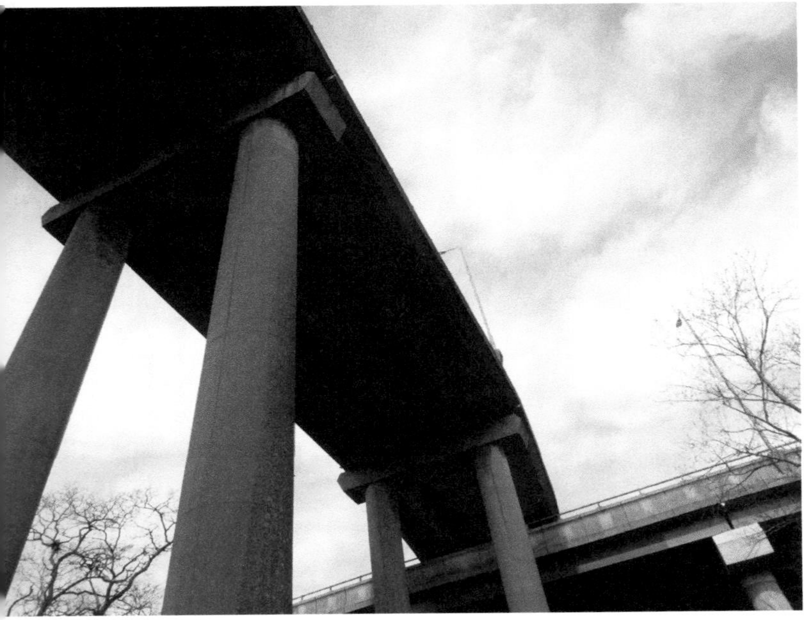

Above: Gravelly Hill Interchange is known by the nickname Spaghetti Junction.

Left: The concrete structure is an amazing feat of civil engineering.

National polls on more than one occasion have branded Gravelly Hill intersection as the most intimidating road system in Great Britain, although a quarter of a million cars use Spaghetti Junction every day with no navigation problems.

More than fifty years after it was opened, Spaghetti Junction remains an outstanding piece of civil engineering. It is built over five levels and supported on 500 concrete columns of 100 feet in height. There are 2 miles of slipways leading to eighteen different roads, all intermixed with various railway, canal and river routes. When positioning the support columns, allowance was made for access for horse-drawn canal boats on the towpaths, although the site is rarely visited by anything but the cars which pass overhead.

47. Alpha Tower (1973)

The Alpha Tower is in the heart of Birmingham overlooking Centenary Square. At twenty-eight storeys it is the tallest office block in the city and has been Grade II listed by Historic England.

This accolade was fought for by the Twentieth Century Society, who first proposed the building for listing in 2002. The owners of the Alpha Tower at the time feared that the regulations that affect listed properties would diminish their financial investment but their attempts to get an Immunity from Listing certificate failed.

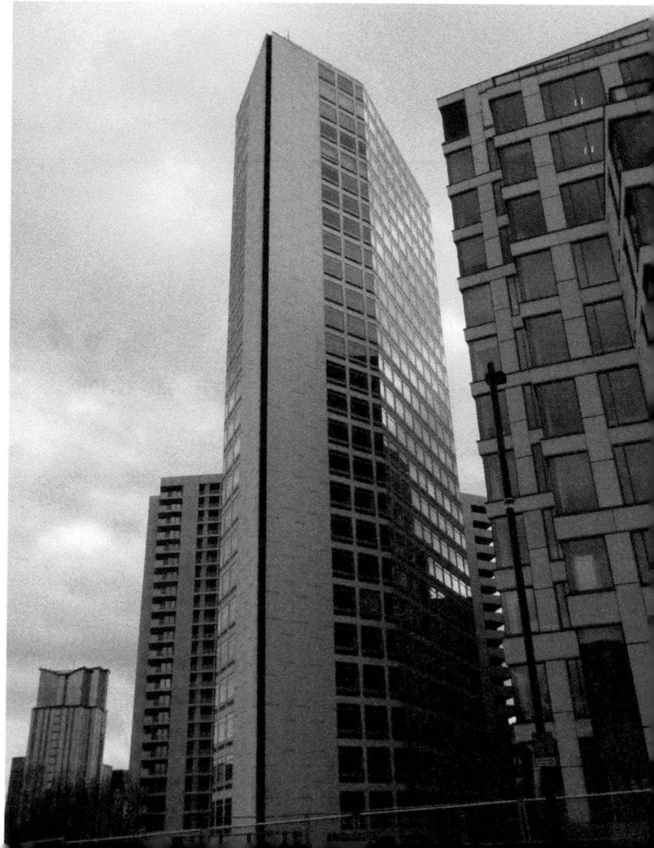

Modernist in style, the Alpha Tower was built in 1973.

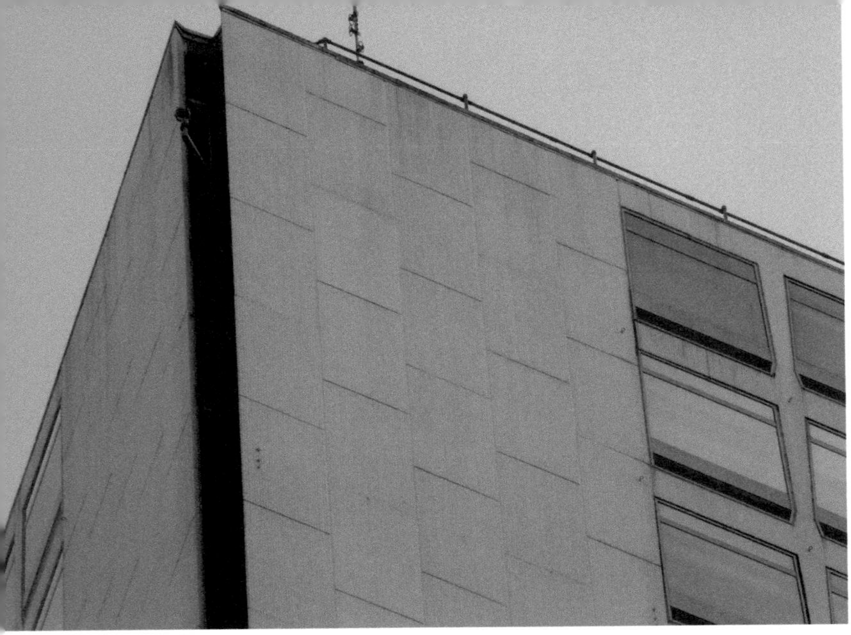

The building has been designed with stylish shaping.

The modernist-style Alpha Tower took three years to build and opened in 1973 as the headquarters for ATV, the main television company in the Midlands. When ATV closed in 1982, the property was leased by Birmingham City Council until it was purchased by a private company in 2010.

The architect of the building was Birmingham-born George Marsh, who was a leading figure in office block design. It was the aesthetics of the building that eventually persuaded English Heritage to list it. They admired Marsh's carefully detailed design with its elegant shaped outline. In a poll, Birmingham residents agreed, voting the 328-foot-tall Alpha Tower a favourite commercial building.

The block is constructed using a reinforced concrete frame set with a regular pattern of aluminium framed windows and clad in white. The footprint of the tower is banana shaped, and the gentle curve tapers to a tessellated mosaic edge. The ground floor has a colonnade of geometric pillars topped by a lintel, which gives the illusion of supporting the whole building.

The Grade II listing does not include the interior and it has been modernised many times. However, it retains the open-plan vision of the architect and natural light is still able to flood through the windows and into the lobby on each floor.

48. Selfridge's Building (2003)

When Harry Selfridge opened the first department store in Great Britain, he declared that 'shopping should be a great and sensual pleasure'. He had realised that it was the shopping environment that attracted consumers as much as the products on offer. The innovative flagship building of the regenerated Bullring Shopping Centre is a part of the Selfridge's heritage and also provides a unique customer environment for its clientele.

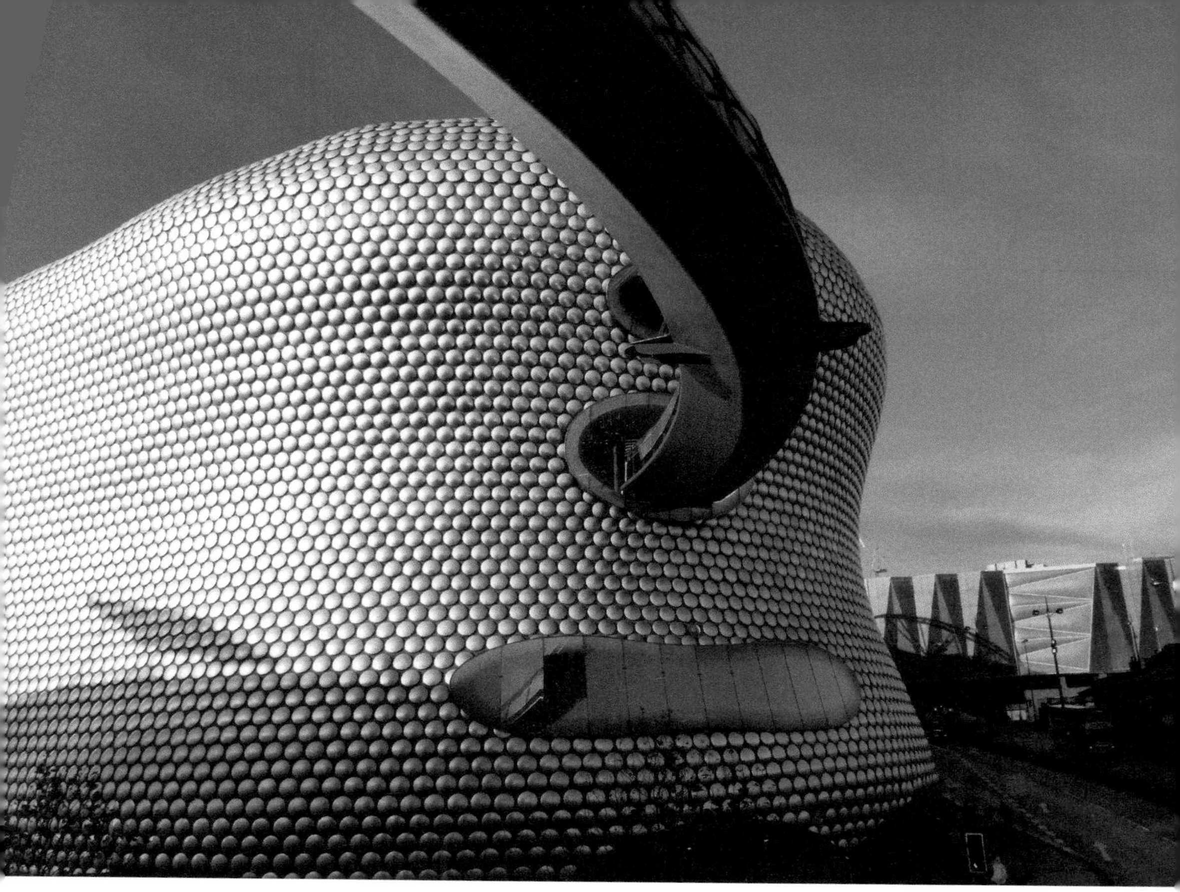

Selfridges flagship store devised its own style of architecture.

The £60 million Selfridge's building was designed by Jan Kaplicky & Amanda Levete in 2003 and opened the same year. In 2004, the building won the Award for Architectural Merit given by the Royal Institute of British Architects and it has consistently been recognised as one of the best stores in the world to visit.

The Selfridge company wanted their new shop to be distinctive, and the design submitted was so innovative that a new term for its style of architecture was created. New York journalist William Safire was producing an article about the building and he could find no word to describe the undulating shape, which he had previously likened to an amoeba. He entitled his article 'The Rise of Blobitecture', and the term has now been coined for subsequent similar designs.

Other descriptions of the Selfridge's building have concluded that it looks either oceanic or extra-terrestrial and that the connection bridge could be likened to the proboscis of an insect. The design draws on elements of air, earth and water to produce the appearance of movement. The 15,000 aluminium discs of the outer shell reflect the sky, the weather and anything that passes by. This causes the colour to change constantly and evokes a feeling of fluidity and motion.

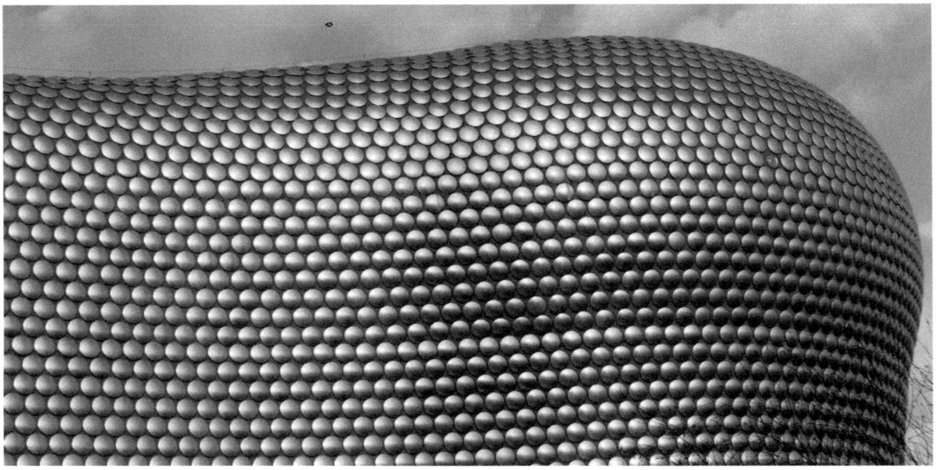

Reflective aluminium cladding makes the building appear to change colour.

The building has a steel frame with a concrete façade and a metallic top shell to which the discs are attached. Inside, the four shopping levels are accessed using the round white escalator shaft, which is a central feature of the interior design.

49. Beetham Tower (2006)

The definition of a skyscraper is of a building that is over forty floors and 330 feet high. The Beetham Tower is nearly 400 feet tall and has forty-one storeys, which officially makes it the only skyscraper in Birmingham.

The building was designed by architect Ian Simpson, who wanted the construction to be a postmodernist representation of the spirit of the technological age. The gently curved façade is clad completely in delicately patterned glass. The stripes of blue in the glass make the building appear to reflect the sky and create an atmospheric light. Coloured illuminations highlight the top after dark. The apartments in the Beetham Tower have spectacular views and received a housing design award in 2006.

The three-year construction of the concrete tower created problems for traffic on the surrounding ring road. Some of the scaffolding collapsed and sheets of both cladding and glass fell into the road causing major congestion on various occasions. After the building was opened there were issues with the computer-controlled underground car park. Residents drive their car onto a platform and a computerised process takes the vehicle to a space. It is retrieved when the resident wants their car back. Software failure left drivers unable to access their vehicles for up to a week at a time before the issue was rectified.

Many photographs of the Beetham Tower show it with the Chinese pagoda that stands on Holloway Circus Roundabout in the foreground. The pagoda

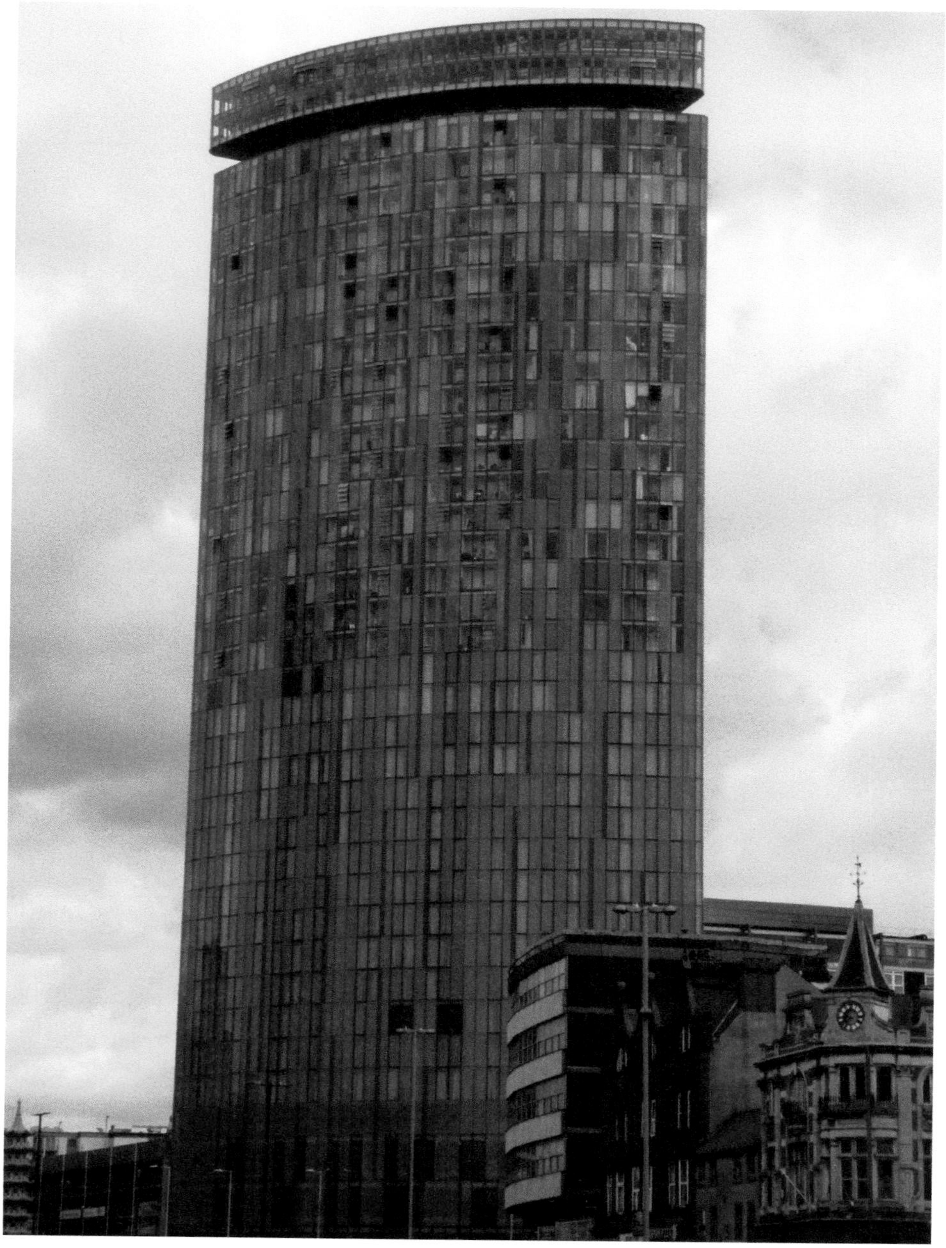

The skyscraper is constructed using steel and blue glass.

was presented by a local businessman in 1998 to symbolise the traditions of Birmingham's nearby Chinese Quarter. Although the pagoda appears to be dominated by the Beetham Tower, the modern glass building and the traditional granite monument subtly contrast and complement each other. The Royal Institute

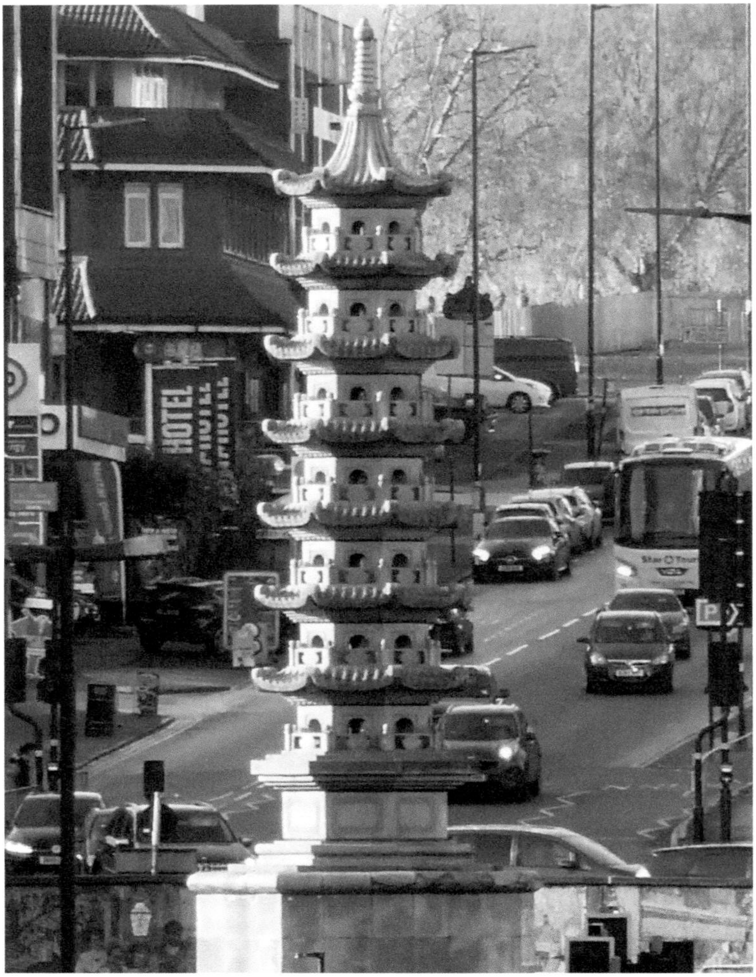

The pagoda is an architectural example of Birmingham's diversity.

of British Architects have commended the architect for creating a sculptural building that is symbolic of the ambition and confidence of Birmingham's ongoing urban regeneration while recognising its heritage.

50. Library of Birmingham (2013)

The first public library in Great Britain was founded in Birmingham in 1635. There were three more libraries built for the city in subsequent years but each proved too small and larger premises were sought on every occasion.

The Library of Birmingham is now a colourful, high-tech, postmodernist building on Centenary Square. It was designed by Dutch architect Francine Houben in 2013 and adds to the eclectic architectural designs in the area.

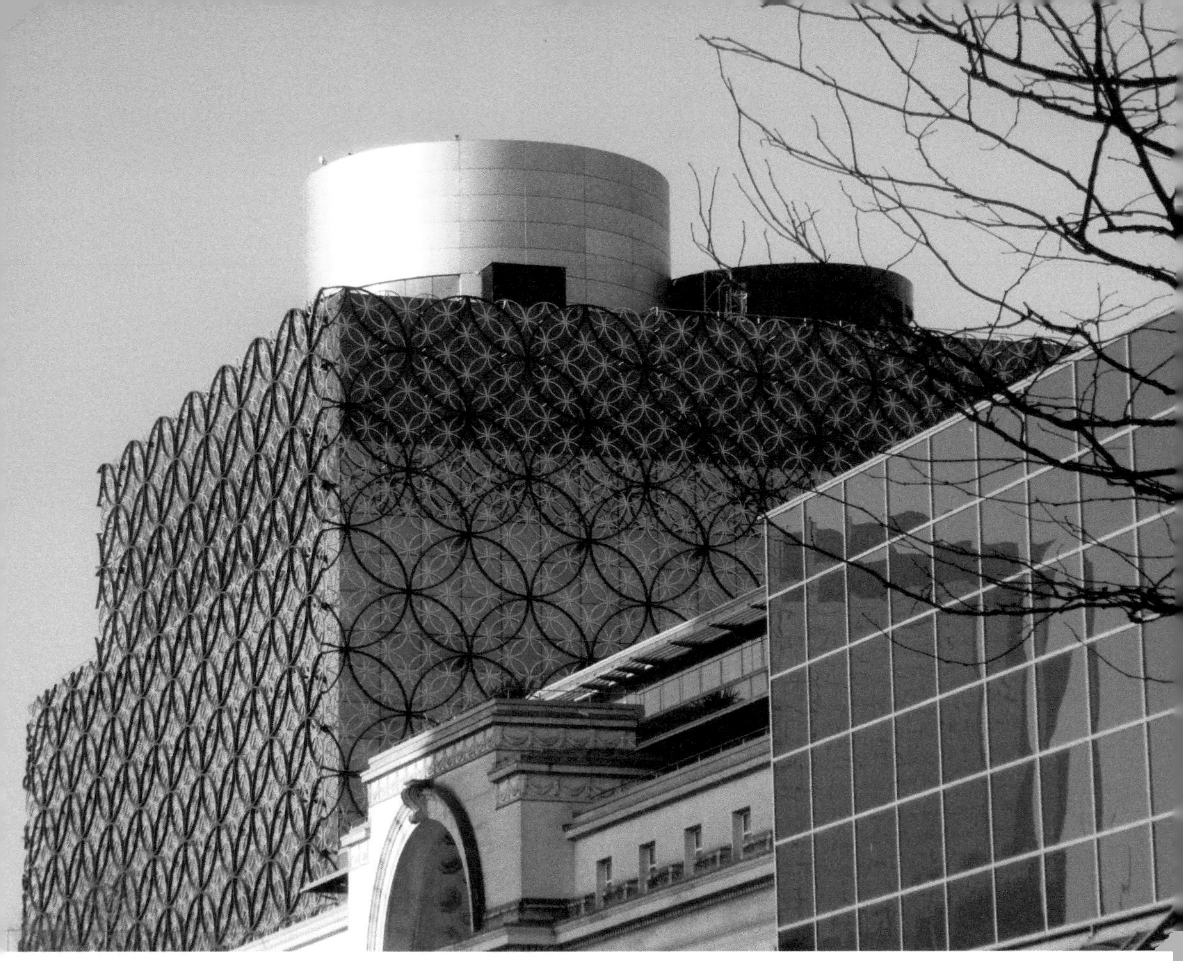

The Library of Birmingham has an important Shakespeare collection.

The library has ten levels. The cantilevered first floor acts as a canopy for the ground floor restaurant where it opens onto Centenary Square, and an upper storey has become a garden terrace with spectacular views over the city. On the roof is a rotunda housing the Shakespeare Memorial Room. This reading room contains the library's accumulation of material by William Shakespeare and the whole interior has been preserved and moved from previous libraries within the city. The Library of Birmingham's most valuable book is part of the collection and is a copy of Shakespeare's First Folio from 1623, which is estimated to be worth £7 million.

The building has been constructed using concrete and glass and has layers of beige and grey blocks. The façade is covered with an iconic filigree of aluminium rings, which were each individually placed into position.

The key theme of the library is circles. The round shapes have been designed to represent Birmingham's industrial past and refer to gasometers, canal tunnels and arched viaducts. The interior similarly has a circular theme. The interior spaces have curving walls and the main atrium forms a ring around the stairwell. The central hall features a wall of books, which line it from floor to ceiling.

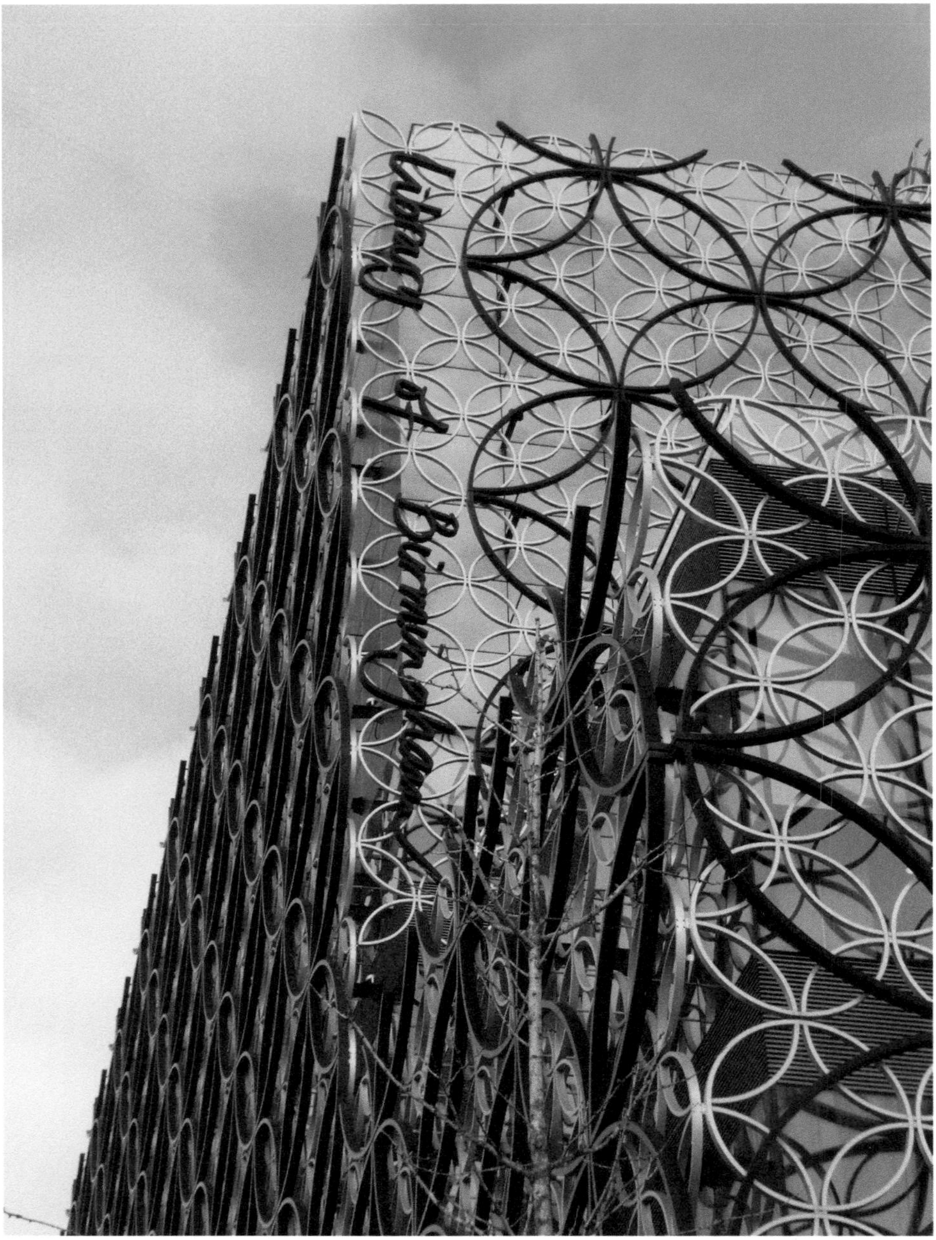

Intricate filigree work incorporates the building's theme of circles.

The first book to be placed on the shelves of the Library of Birmingham was a copy of *The Hobbit* by J. R. R. Tolkien. The author had lived locally in his younger years and much of the inspiration for his visualisation of Middle Earth came from sites around the city. There is an unofficial trail that visits these sites.